Integrating Women's Studies
into the Curriculum

Integrating Women's Studies into the Curriculum

A Guide and Bibliography

Betty Schmitz

The Feminist Press
Old Westbury, New York

Library of Congress Cataloging in Publication Data

Schmitz, Betty.
  Integrating women's studies into the curriculum.

  Bibliography: p.
  Includes index.
  1. Women's studies—United States—Congresses.
2. Interdisciplinary approach in education—United
States—Congresses. 3. Education, Humanistic—
United States—Curricula—Congresses. 4. Universities
and colleges—United States—Curricula—Congresses.
I. Title.
HQ1181.U5S36 1985   378.'199'0973   84-28638
ISBN 0-935312-36-6 (pbk.)

Cover and text design by Lucinda C. Geist
Typeset by Weinglas Typography Co. Inc.
Manufactured by Haddon Craftsmen, Inc.

Activities reported in this book were performed pursuant to a grant from
the Fund for the Improvement of Postsecondary Education, U.S. Department of Education. However, the opinions expressed herein do not necessarily reflect the position or policy of the U.S. Department of Education
and no official endorsement by the Department should be inferred.

Prepared in partial fulfillment of Grant #G008102311

Contents

Foreword

The past 15 years have witnessed the dramatic growth of women's studies in the United States. Today, there are more than 480 women's studies programs in colleges and universities across the country. Thousands of scholarly works have been published. More than 100 campus-based faculty development projects have focused on changing the main undergraduate curriculum with new materials and perspectives from women's studies.

Certain features of feminist scholarship have made these curriculum change projects unusually complex. First, because new research on women and feminist perspectives on existing knowledge encompass all academic disciplines, this scholarship is difficult to assimilate. Second, the interdisciplinary nature of women's studies requires basic structural changes in methods of organizing and imparting knowledge. The new scholarship on women cannot be used simply to amplify existing course programs. Rather, it requires revision and correction and, in some cases, transformation of existing bodies of knowledge.

For some years, directors of faculty development projects have been exchanging information informally on how best to do this work. Until now, no comprehensive guide to successful project management existed.

This book answers the need. *Integrating Women's Studies into the Curriculum* is a thorough, practical guide for all faculty and administrators who have come to realize that the male-defined college curriculum is obsolete. By illuminating proven patterns of formal collegial support, Betty Schmitz clears the way for faculty to incorporate the new feminist scholarship into their teaching and their research.

The book deals very specifically with the crucial processes of designing, organizing, initiating, and sustaining projects in a wide variety of institutional settings. It identifies both essential conditions for success and hazards to avoid. It gives advice on overcoming the resistance of faculty who are unconsciously invested in exclusive traditions of scholarship and teaching. And it provides an incisively annotated bibliography and compendious guide to feminist curriculum change projects and resources that will prove valuable for years to come.

Betty Schmitz is the ideal person to have written this book. The guide is based on her experience in directing three major curriculum change programs that have affected dozens of campuses in the United

States. She is particularly aware of the need to structure projects so that faculty motivation remains high, goals remain clear, and both faculty time and administrators' funds are used efficiently. She is respectful of faculty and sensitive to the emotional and intellectual complexities that may develop for teachers engaged in this work, while remaining aware of the practical requirements of projects involving new scholarship on women.

Women's studies as a field is the center and source of vital new interdisciplinary insights. Women's studies programs are growing and must continue to grow. The strategies described here serve equally well to strengthen a women's studies program already in place or to facilitate the formation of a new one. By focusing on the faculty development project itself, this book provides an inestimable direct benefit to faculty: it enables them to make significant changes in their syllabi and their teaching, and therefore pass on to students both more accurate knowledge and more inclusive analytical skills than the present dominant curriculum has ever allowed them to provide.

> Peggy McIntosh, Program Director
> Wellesley College Center for
> Research on Women

Preface

In June 1983, sixty colleges and universities sent representatives to the Wheaton College Conference, "Moving Toward a Balanced Curriculum." Represented at the conference, along with the Wheaton faculty who had participated in a three-year faculty development program aimed at incorporating the new scholarship on women into the liberal arts curriculum, were directors of similar projects at the University of Arizona, the University of Maine at Orono, the University of Massachusetts-Amherst, Montana State University, Lewis and Clark College (Oregon), Smith College, and the Wellesley College Center for Research on Women.

Each of these projects had begun with large external grants from either federal or private sources. One recurring question throughout the three-day conference was how, given cutbacks in funding at the federal and state levels, colleges and universities could initiate new projects to integrate women's studies into the liberal arts curriculum. Project leaders wondered what was realistic to attempt without a sizeable, external grant and how to secure internal resources for curricular change.

Integrating Women's Studies into the Curriculum is written in response to such questions and to a growing interest on campuses across the country in transforming the curriculum through incorporation of the new scholarship on women. It complements recent collections of essays on feminist transformation of the curriculum, such as those by Langland and Gove (see Part Three, #41), Sherman and Beck (#18), Spanier et al. (#62), and Spender (#20), that treat theoretical issues of curricular change both generally and in relation to specific disciplines by addressing practical questions about project management.

My sense of what is necessary for a successful project to incorporate feminist scholarship into the main curriculum comes primarily from the two curriculum integration projects I directed at Montana State University. In the first of these, funded between 1979 and 1981 by the Women's Educational Equity Act (WEEA) Program, I worked with forty Montana State University faculty in both the liberal arts and professional schools who conducted research on women and revised courses they regularly taught. The strategies and results of this project were extended to ten postsecondary institutions in Idaho, Montana, Utah, and Wyoming through the second project, the Northern Rockies Program on Women in the Curriculum, funded by the Fund for the Improvement of Postsecondary Education, 1981–83. In contrast to the WEEA Project, which was funded at approximately $180,000 for each of two years, each institution participating in the Northern Rockies Program received minimal assistance to initiate a curriculum integration project: a four-day training institute (to which participants paid their own way), a resource notebook, and $2,000 in matching funds. The diverse strategies these ten institutions brought to bear on curricular reform provide concrete examples of how to initiate and sustain a project with modest resources.

My recommendations for program development also reflect numerous discussions with faculty and administrators attempting to initiate projects at their institutions and my visits to other campuses around the country engaged in integrating women's studies into the curriculum, particularly the University of Arizona, Lewis and Clark College (Oregon), Portland Community College, Purdue University, Moorhead State University, and Eastern Washington University. My thinking has been further informed by sharing experiences with other project directors at meetings such as the Workshop on Integrating Women's Studies into the Curriculum sponsored by the Southwest Institute for Research on Women (SIROW) in August 1981 (see Part Three, Dinnerstein et al., #30), the Wheaton Conference, and at National Women's Studies Association meetings.

Integrating Women's Studies into the Curriculum contains three parts. The first part describes the process of implementing a project aimed at transforming the general curriculum through incorporation of insights from women's studies research and teaching. Drawing upon the experience of the Northern Rockies Program and similar projects, it addresses questions such as how to assess the institutional climate for change; how to plan, initiate, and sustain a project; and how to deal with resistance to change. It provides pragmatic strategies and recommendations for people interested in beginning projects.

Part Two contains brief histories, arranged by type of project, of the ten projects that participated in the Northern Rockies Program on Women in the Curriculum. For each project history, information on institutional setting, project goals, plan of action, short-term impact, and the project director is provided. To provide a larger compendium of change strategies, these histories are complemented by inclusion of an annotated combined listing of the 1984 Wellesley College Center for Research on Women *Directory of Projects* and a listing of the projects funded by the Western States Project on Women in the Curriculum.

Part Three is an annotated bibliography providing references to theoretical works, reports, programs, curriculum materials, resources, and organizations available to assist in the development of a project to integrate women's studies into the curriculum. It was compiled chiefly through the reading and reviewing of such periodicals as *Signs* (#138), the *Women's Studies Quarterly* (#145), *On Campus with Women* (see #207), and *Feminist Collections* (#124). I learned of many of the more recent unpublished or forthcoming materials through my work as Coordinator of the Clearinghouse for Curriculum Integration Projects at Montana State University. The main focus of the bibliography is on works dealing specifically with curriculum. However, since the politics of the curriculum are directly related to the status of women on campus, several sources on women as students and employees are included. Annotations are descriptive rather than evaluative. References are, for the most part, to materials and resources published since 1978; the end date for the literature search was January 1984, with only a few major additions for the remainder of 1984. Readers are referred to Esther Stineman's *Women's Studies: A Recommended Core Bibliography* (#173) and Patricia Ballou's *Women: A Bibliography of Bibliographies* (#148) for earlier works in women's studies. In some cases, nonpublished materials are listed if they are readily available through an established organization.

For the reader's convenience, references in the text to works listed in the bibliography are made to the numerical designation of the item (i.e., Dinnerstein et al., #30). Author and subject indexes to works listed in the bibliography and a directory of publishers may be found at the back of the book.

Acknowledgments

Many people contributed to this book in important ways. I wish to thank first and foremost the project directors who participated in the Northern Rockies Program on Women in the Curriculum: for their energy, their commitment, their willingness to provide information and materials, and for their insight and candor in describing their projects. My program officers at the Fund for the Improvement of Postsecondary Education, Leslie Hornig and Carol Stoel, provided assistance and guidance throughout the two-year program. Linda Shadiow, assistant project director, co-authored the grant proposal and contributed energy and creativity to the project. Anne Williams designed the evaluation plan, collected and analyzed data, and made essential recommendations for managing the project and interpreting the results. I also wish to express my appreciation to Florence Howe, who encouraged me to write this book; to Kathy Harte, who lived through the writing of the first draft and gave me constant support; and to Elaine Reuben, who read that draft and made very helpful revisions and suggestions. Corky Bush, Diane Sands, and JoAnn Fritsche read and commented on later versions of the main text, and Sara Jayne Steen assisted me with the bibliography. I am also grateful to Myra Dinnerstein and Nancy Porter, who were always willing to discuss pressing issues and offer solutions. Peggy McIntosh, Marilyn Schuster, and Susan Van Dyne also contributed important insights and support at critical moments. I thank both Peggy and Barbara Kneubuhl for providing their *Directory of Projects* for inclusion in Section 7. Finally, I wish to acknowledge and thank Jo Baird, my editor at The Feminist Press, for her invaluable assistance.

Introduction
Women's Studies in the Academy

The Development of Women's Studies

As early as 1968, women were beginning to document the existence of sex bias in educational institutions and to develop courses to compensate for the lack of information on women in the curriculum. From the outset, women's studies had two explicit goals: to develop a body of knowledge and a new curriculum that focus on women and gender; and to use this new knowledge to transform the male-centered curriculum of educational institutions. The first decade of women's studies concentrated on the former goal, with phenomenal results.

In 1972, the first issue of the *Women's Studies Newsletter* reported the existence of forty-six women's studies programs, of which six offered a baccalaureate degree in women's studies. By 1984, the Women's Studies Program Directory contained more than ten times as many programs, including 247 baccalaureate programs, 55 master's programs, and 21 doctoral programs.[1] This represents one program for every six institutions of higher education in the United States. There are some forty centers for research on women affiliated with the National Council for Research on Women; a strong and growing professional association, the National Women's Studies Association; women's caucuses in most of the professional, discipline-based associations; and several academic journals devoted to women's studies theory and practice.

The body of knowledge embodied in the mature women's studies curriculum already represents a formidable amount of material that crosses the boundaries of traditional disciplines.[2] The women's studies curriculum varies from institution to institution, depending on administrative arrangements and the availability of faculty to teach courses. At a minimum, the curriculum includes an Introduction to Women's Studies and a series of departmentally based courses such as Women in Literature, Psychology of Sex Roles, or Feminism and Philosophy. A mature program with a line budget and paid administrator might also offer a variety of senior seminars on aspects of feminist theory and field work practica, as well as intermediate-level interdisciplinary courses to supplement departmental offerings.

In addition to a growing body of scholarship, women's studies brings to the academy a new pedagogy that seeks to break down hi-

1

erarchical modes of teaching and to empower students to take responsibility for their own learning. In the women's studies classroom, the experience of the individual student is explicitly sought and valued and provides a base of experiential information that complements textual material. A conscious attempt is made to focus on issues of race and class, as well as gender, and as women's studies continues to grow in the 1980s, the reexamination and revision of its existing curriculum to ensure that it is inclusive of women of differing races, cultures, economic classes, and sexual identity are major emphases.

The Emergence of Curriculum Integration
as a Change Strategy

Despite the veritable explosion of knowledge about women and gender and the development of courses to teach this new material and method, the majority of students still graduate from American colleges and universities without any exposure to this scholarship or to the feminist analysis of society and culture that women's studies provides. Assessments of the impact of women's studies on the campus and the disciplines indicate that little progress has been made in altering traditional world views as presented in courses outside of the women's studies curriculum. Syllabi, for the most part, have remained unchanged and textbooks appearing in the 1980s still omit considerations of women and gender and perpetuate traditional biases.[3] Incorporation of insights from feminist scholarship and teaching into courses outside of women's studies has until very recently been carried out primarily by women's studies faculty teaching standard courses within their disciplines. The goal to which many women's studies faculty and scholars are hence now turning, in more systematic ways than in the past, is the transformation of the "main" curriculum. Individual campuses, through a variety of approaches and strategies, and often with the added impetus of new priorities from funding agencies sensitive to equity concerns,[4] are developing programs with the explicit goal of expanding the impact of women's studies throughout the institution.

Since the mid-1970s, Guilford College, a coeducational institution in Greensboro, North Carolina, and Stephens, a women's college in Columbia, Missouri, have been promoting and encouraging the integration of material about women into the liberal arts curriculum through faculty development activities. In 1976, the Wellesley College Center for Research on Women instituted, with the aid of the Mellon Foundation, a grant program for New England faculty to explore ways of changing the knowledge base of the traditional disciplines to incorporate feminist scholarship. In 1979, three major projects were funded by the Women's Educational Equity Act Program: Georgia State University received a grant to develop a model program for "gender-balancing the curriculum in higher education" and established a network of Southern scholars doing feminist research on transforming the curriculum; Utah State University to develop content guides for teaching about women in introductory courses in economics, psychology, and sociology; and the Montana State University Project to provide stipends for faculty to conduct research on women and revise courses in the standard curriculum. That same year, the Fund for the Improvement of Postsecondary Education funded the Organization of American Historians to develop materials to integrate women's history into standard courses in Western civilization and United States history. In 1981, with support from the Lilly Foundation, the Great Lakes Colleges Association Women's Studies Program sponsored their first national summer institute "Toward a Feminist Transformation of the Academy," an idea that had been in the planning stages since 1978.

Directors of such projects as these began to compare approaches and strategies for change and to present what they had learned to others at meetings sponsored by funding agencies and at conferences of the National Women's Studies Association. The 1980 NWSA Conference in Bloomington, Indiana featured five sessions on incorporating feminist scholarship into the curriculum. It was, however, the impetus provided by two national invitational conferences in 1981 that served to formalize the new curricular change movement.

The Workshop on Integrating Women's Studies into the Curriculum was organized and sponsored by the Southwest Institute for Research on Women (SIROW), with support from the Rockefeller Family Fund and the National Endowment for the Humanities, in Princeton, New Jersey, August 27–30, 1981. At this meeting, directors of seventeen projects, faculty from the social sciences and humanities, and representatives of major funding agencies convened to exchange information and strategies on integrating women's studies into the curriculum, assess current theory and practice, and develop a paper to inform college administrators about the goals and potential impact of such projects. Participants represented a variety of approaches to curricular change and a wide spectrum of institutional settings: there were four women's colleges (Smith, Stephens, Wellesley, Wheaton); seven state universities (Arizona, California State at Hayward, Georgia State, Maine at Orono, Massachusetts, Montana State, and North Dakota); two religious colleges (Guilford and Saint Mary's); one coeducational liberal arts college (Lewis and Clark in Oregon); two college consortia (the Great Lakes Colleges Association and the Sixteen-College Informal Coalition); and one discipline-specific project (Reconstructing American Literature, The

Feminist Press). At this meeting directors of programs began to realize the extent of the movement underway and its potential for impact on the traditional curriculum.

The impetus for these projects varied considerably.[5] Universities
with strong women's studies programs, such as Arizona and
California State at Hayward, had undertaken faculty development
programs with the intent of increasing the numbers of students exposed to the new scholarship on women. St. Mary's and Denison
were working to influence the revision of the general education requirements to include courses on women and minorities. At Smith,
Stephens, and Georgia State, faculty, drawn together initially
through mutual research interests, began to explore ways of integrating the new scholarship on women into the curriculum. Still
other projects, like the Wellesley College Center for Research on
Women Faculty Development Program and the Project on Reconstructing American Literature, aimed to reevaluate the traditional
knowledge bases of the disciplines and transform them to incorporate the study of class, race, and gender. The common goal of these
projects, however, as described by Peggy McIntosh in the introduction to the *Directory of Projects: Transforming the Liberal Arts Curriculum Through Incorporation of the New Scholarship on Women*, was to
"help faculty in traditional disciplines to use the key research findings, fresh perspectives, and transforming insights which arise from
the new scholarship on women."[6]

The SIROW report for administrators generated by the Princeton
Workshop was written expressly for dissemination at the second
major national conference—The Wingspread Conference on "Liberal
Education and the New Scholarship on Women: Issues and Constraints in Institutional Change," sponsored by the Association of
American Colleges with support from the Ford, Lilly, and Johnson
Foundations, and held in Racine, Wisconsin, October 22–24, 1981.[7]
This invitational conference had a two-fold purpose: to consider the
implications of the new scholarship on women for the traditional
goals and assumptions of liberal education, and to challenge the
larger educational community into serious consideration of impera-
tives for curricular and institutional change. Participants met as a
policy-making body and generated a series of recommendations for
administrators, faculty, and professional associations. This was the
first time that a group of college administrators dedicated themselves to learning about women's studies scholarship and the need
to transform the liberal arts curriculum. This added visibility among
administrators provided further impetus to the movement.

Other opportunities and structures emerged to support the
growth and development of the movement. In 1982, the Wellesley

College Center for Research on Women received another grant from the Mellon Foundation to support a National Consulting Program and a National Fellowship Program. The Center also instituted a Black Women's Studies Faculty and Curriculum Development Program, published the first *Directory of Projects*, which listed forty-two projects, and developed a list of consultants to assist institutions in initiating projects. That spring, at the National Women's Studies Association meeting at Humboldt State University, representatives of twelve projects formed a Task Force on Curriculum Integration. The Task Force meets annually and coordinates panels at NWSA and has established a clearinghouse for the dissemination of non-published materials, such as syllabi, reports, and conference agendas.[8] The *Women's Studies Quarterly* also began reporting on the development of this movement.[9] In 1983, SIROW and Montana State University received a grant from the Ford Foundation to establish the Western States Project on Women in the Curriculum and provide small grants for project development to four-year institutions in a sixteen-state region.[10]

The attendance of 200 faculty and administrators representing 60 institutions at the Wheaton College Conference in June 1983 and the funding of two dozen projects by the Western States Project in 1983–84 indicate that the number of institutions with established curriculum integration projects will continue to grow. With this growth comes the necessity to assess the goals of these programs in relation to women's studies and their potential impact on the future of feminism within higher education.

The Question of Strategy

At the Wheaton College Conference, the 1982 and 1983 NWSA Conventions, and in various women's studies journals and newsletters, serious concerns about the curriculum integration movement have been raised by women's studies scholars and activists as they consider strategies to support the continuing development and expansion of women's studies programs and scholarship in a period of shrinking resources and institutional retrenchment.[11] These concerns are well founded. The curriculum integration movement emerges in a period of tight resources, but also at a time when many women's studies programs are attempting to move into what Florence Howe has called "phase three": a program with tenured staff, adequate administrative arrangements, and a permanent curriculum.[12] Women's studies faculty fear that administrators may embrace integration as an alternative to hiring and tenuring women's studies faculty or as an argument for terminating or cutting back women's studies offerings. In terms of personal survival, women's studies faculty wonder how they will continue to do the research and teaching necessary to achieve tenure and promotion while undertaking the re-education of their previously recalcitrant peers.

The experience of curriculum integration projects varies on these points. Administrators who have become aware of the new effort have frequently responded to program development as an "either-or" choice between women's studies and curriculum integration.[13] There have been cases where administrators have sponsored consultancies and faculty development workshops and used integration of the study of women throughout the curriculum as an argument for reallocating institutional resources and eliminating women's studies faculty. At some institutions, women's studies faculty do not control the funds being used to introduce new faculty to women's studies scholarship and have not been consulted in the planning process for such programs. Yet many institutions report that faculty development projects have increased the legitimacy of women's studies on campus, developed new advocacy groups for women's studies, resulted in the hiring of new feminist faculty, increased the numbers of women's studies courses in the curriculum, strengthened degree programs, or, in some cases, led directly to the creation of or the refunding of a women's studies program.[14]

Another central area of concern about integration centers on the problem of the quality of the work being produced. Directors of curriculum integration projects have themselves noted the uneven quality of much of the initial course revision work done by faculty: many simply add a new unit on women to an otherwise unreconstructed course with no attempt to question the underlying assumptions of the discipline. Critics of the integration movement also suggest that the least radical scholarship may be selected for faculty development seminars precisely because it is the most acceptable to the hoped-for converts and that these programs may have the effect of diluting rather than strengthening feminism in the academy. What, they wonder, is being passed on to students by these as-yet-unconverted faculty? How can the full complexity and scope of feminist scholarship, which transcends disciplinary boundaries, be integrated into a traditional, discipline-based course? Equally critical questions are the extent to which feminist pedagogy informs teaching in the "integrated classroom" and the degree to which those directing the change efforts become the ones who are themselves changed.[15]

Other agendas appear much more worthy of slim resources and limited energies. Not the least of these is the enrichment of feminist scholarship and the further development of women's studies as a field. Women's studies is only beginning to develop a multicultural, inclusive perspective in content and methodology. Hence, as Johnnella Butler has noted, women's studies must transform itself before it can represent for the rest of the academy the truth about human experience.[16]

Terminology

The question about the best strategy for maintaining a feminist presence in the academy extends to the names applied to the new faculty development projects. One of the earliest terms was "mainstreaming women's studies," chosen to convey the goal of expanding the reach of women's studies into areas central to the curriculum of every student. This term, however, has been abandoned because of its undesirable connotations. As Peggy McIntosh points out, the term trivializes women and women's studies by implying that women are marginal and further suggests that feminist studies can be easily absorbed by the traditional disciplines.[17]

The 1981 SIROW report was entitled *How to Integrate Women's Studies into the Curriculum.* The abbreviated phrase "curriculum integration" was subsequently adopted by the NWSA Task Force on Curriculum Integration. Some also find this name undesirable because it, like mainstreaming, implies women's studies can be integrated into the disciplines as they currently stand, and further that women's studies has not been a legitimate part of the higher education curriculum. To avoid these implications, others have chosen to use the term "curriculum transformation," which better conveys the ultimate goal if not the state-of-the-art of these projects, or to use descriptive alternatives, such as projects to transform the liberal arts curriculum through incorporation of the new scholarship on women. Still others have selected project names with an eye toward campus politics, calling themselves projects to "balance the curriculum," or to "gender-balance the curriculum." Yet these names may confuse faculty attempting to understand the content and methodology of feminist scholarship and its implications for course revision by implying that a certain proportion of material is required in order to "balance" a course.

Gender-balancing, along with integrating or incorporating women's studies (or the new scholarship on women) into the curriculum, remain common titles applied to the faculty development projects.[18] By choosing the title *Integrating Women's Studies into the Curriculum* for this book, I am recognizing that women's studies is the root of this curricular reform movement and is essential to its continued success. The term women's studies embodies the feminist and transformative nature of the new scholarship on women. It is broader than the term "new scholarship on women" in that it also incorporates the practice of teaching this new scholarship. I use the term "curriculum" to refer to the general curriculum in higher education, not solely the liberal arts curriculum. Finally, I chose the verb "integrate," despite its problematic implications, to describe how change is initiated, and not to convey the ultimate goal, which remains the transformation of structures of knowledge and of educational institutions.

One Agenda: Multiple Strategies

Cognizant of the serious ideological and political issues, proponents of the curriculum integration movement, of which I am obviously one, see women's studies and curriculum integration as two points on a continuum or two versions of the same work, one carried out primarily with students, the other with faculty colleagues. The faculty development projects gain their validity and strength from the radical thinking done in women's studies. The work of introducing faculty to the feminist critique embodied in women's studies, by challenging traditional modes of thinking, shifts the balance slightly and makes more room for the existence of radical thinking within the academy. Critics Marian Lowe and Margaret Lowe Benston, in fact, see a place for integration efforts in challenging antifeminist research and slowing down the current inroads on the few gains feminists have made.[19]

Most of those participating in this discussion acknowledge that work must be done on all fronts at once and that individuals in given institutional settings will choose strategies that make sense within a given political context at a given time. For campuses where women's studies programs currently exist, program staff can elect, if resources exist and priorities demand, to build into their mission statement goals related to bringing about change in the general curriculum: assisting colleagues outside of women's studies to reassess their disciplines and rethink courses, and articulating goals for the study of women throughout departmental curricula. For those campuses without a formalized women's studies program, a faculty development or curricular change project may be the first step, as it was for many of the programs participating in the Northern Rockies Program on Women in the Curriculum, toward developing a women's studies advocacy base from which to work for further change.

Those who continue to conceive of the two strategies as an "either-or" choice should be reminded that the faculty development projects are *based in* rather than *opposed to* women's studies. The goal of these projects is not to create a separate curriculum but to involve more faculty in teaching from a feminist perspective and to expose more students to the new scholarship on women. For decades to come, the place where the knowledge to support this work— feminist scholarship—will be generated will continue to be women's studies programs and research centers.

[handwritten margin note: not just Mission of W.S.]

NOTES
1. "Directory of Women's Studies Programs," *National Women's Studies Association Newsletter* 2,4 (Fall 1984): 27.
2. Florence Howe, "Feminist Scholarship: The Extent of the Revolution," in **#66**, pp. 15–16.
3. See Howe, "Feminist Scholarship"; Howe and Paul Lauter, *The Impact of Women's Studies on the Campus and the Disciplines,***#10**; Lois Banner, Final Report of the Princeton Project on Women in the College Curriculum, 1977. Faculty participating in the Montana State University Women's Educational Equity Act Project, 1979–81, reviewed a total of 124 textbooks in 19 disciplines and found significant omissions and distortions of information on women. [*Research on Women at Montana State University*, 2,1 (Fall 1980).]
4. In 1974 Congress passed the Women's Educational Equity Act establishing a major grant program for model programs to achieve educational equity for women; the National Advisory Council on Women's Educational Programs was created to make policy recommendations to federal education officials on women's educational equity. The Council commissioned the study of women's studies programs, *Seven Years Later*, by Florence Howe (**#73**). In 1979, the National Institute of Education commissioned a series of eight monographs on women's studies following the recommendations Howe outlined in her study. Recommendations for the support of women's studies by the researchers involved in the monograph series were made to the NIE, other federal agencies, and private foundations.
5. Dinnerstein et al., **#30**, pp. 3–4.
6. *Women's Studies Quarterly* 11, 2 (Summer 1983): 23. See also the "Directory of Projects" in Part Two.
7. See *Liberal Education and the New Scholarship on Women*, **#50**.
8. The Task Force on Curriculum Integration is chaired by Myra Dinnerstein, Chair, Women's Studies, University of Arizona; the Clearinghouse for Curriculum Integration disseminates a list of nonpublished project materials, **#170**.
9. Howe, "Editorial: 'What's in a Name?'" 10, 1 (Spring 1982): 2.
10. See Part Two, "Directory of Projects."
11. See the introduction by Bowles and Duelli Klein, *Theories of Women's Studies*, **#2**; *The Women's Studies International Forum*: Special Issue on Strategies for Women's Studies in the 80s, **#22**; Anne Chapman, "Toward Respect for Diversity: Some Hard Questions," *Women's Studies Quarterly* 10, 3 (Fall 1982): 15–16; and my article, "Women's Studies and Projects to Transform the Curriculum: A Current Status Report," **#58**.
12. Howe, *Seven Years Later*, **#73**, p. 67. "Phase one" is a loosely

bound coalition of faculty who work largely on a volunteer basis to offer courses, and "phase two" a program with some formal relationship to the institution, such as a paid administrator, a line budget, and a curriculum recognized in the catalog and approved through regular curriculum committees.

13. See Peggy McIntosh and Elizabeth Minnich, "Varieties of Women's Studies," in #22, p. 143.

14. See my article "A Current Status Report on Curriculum Integration Projects," *Women's Studies Quarterly* 10, 3 (Fall 1982): 16–17; and Bonnie Spanier, "Inside an Integration Project: A Case Study of the Relationship between Balancing the Curriculum and Women's Studies," in #22.

15. This terminology is Helene Wenzel's; see Wenzel and Saj-nicole Joni, "The Changer or the Changed: Feminism in the Universities," in #22; see also Marian Lowe and Margaret Lowe Benston, "The Uneasy Alliance of Feminism and Academia," in #22.

16. "Minority Studies and Women's Studies: Do We Want to Kill a Dream?" in #22.

17. Peggy McIntosh, "A Note on Terminology," *Women's Studies Quarterly* 11, 2 (Spring 1983): 29–30; see also Mary Childers, "Working Definition of a Balanced Course," in the same issue, pp. 30–31; Howe, "What's in a Name?" in the same issue; and McIntosh and Minnich, "Varieties of Women's Studies," in #22.

18. Throughout this book I have used interchangeably the phrases feminist scholarship, women's studies scholarship, and the new scholarship on women; I also frequently use the abbreviated term "curriculum integration" to describe projects. My terminology varies from place to place, however, since I have been influenced by what project leaders themselves choose to call their projects.

19. Lowe and Benston in #22.

PART ONE

Approaches to Project Management

1

Studies in Change

The ten institutions participating in the Northern Rockies Program on Women in the Curriculum initiated projects with minimal budgets compared to many of their predecessors, which had major grants from federal agencies or private foundations. They hence had to fashion goals and activities for smaller scale efforts and rely primarily on internal commitment. Their collective experiences—their strategies and results, their successes and failures—form the basis for the approaches to project implementation recommended in the following sections of this book.

This section provides the context for these local efforts. It describes the goals, strategies, and results of the Montana State University faculty development project for the purpose of providing a point of departure and comparison for the Northern Rockies projects. The rationale, goals, and strategies of the Northern Rockies Program are also presented.[1]

Individual project histories of the ten participating institutions are found in Part Two.

THE MONTANA STATE UNIVERSITY PROJECT

Montana State University, a state-supported, land-grant institution enrolling about 11,000 students, has never had a women's studies program. It became, however, one of the first institutions to involve a large number of faculty in integrating the study of women and gender into standard courses. The Montana State University Project, funded by the Women's Educational Equity Act (WEEA) Program, was a two-year faculty development program aimed at reducing bias in postsecondary curriculum. Forty faculty participants from the university's seven schools and colleges were selected in a competitive process to receive grants for course revision. These eighteen women and twenty-two men represented twenty-five of the university's forty-two departments, including disciplines in the liberal arts and professional areas of arts and architecture, agriculture, business, engineering, and nursing.

The MSU Project supported these forty faculty participants for the two-year period in an intensive effort to provide them with an understanding of the nature and extent of curricular bias in higher education and to introduce them to feminist scholarship in their respective

13

disciplines. In this it differed from similar projects, such as those at Wheaton College and the University of Arizona, which have selected a new group of participants each year. Resources to support individual faculty research and development activities included a $1,500 yearly stipend and clerical and library search assistance. Project funds provided Montana State University with a fully-staffed program office charged with developing faculty expertise in women's studies and improving campus resources to support teaching about women in the disciplines. The project staff consisted of a full-time director, a full-time administrative assistant, a half-time secretary, and a half-time research assistant. (This is much more, it is worth observing, than women's studies programs are normally able to allocate for program administration.)

A major aim of the project was to produce a series of discipline-specific essays written by faculty about the process and results of course revision. Faculty development seminars and project activities were hence geared toward this end. In an Orientation Workshop in January 1980, Myra Sadker and David Sadker of the School of Education of American University presented a model for analysis of sex bias in textbooks, course content, and classroom interaction; this seminar was followed in February by a second one on bias in science by Lilli Hornig of the Wellesley College Center for Research on Women. In April, Sheila Tobias, then Visiting Professor of Women's Studies, Vanderbilt University, presented an overview of women's studies approaches to curriculum development, with examples from the disciplines of literature, history, and physics. In conjunction with these seminars, faculty participants reviewed the content of their courses for sex bias, conducted literature reviews, and initiated research projects with a view toward course revision. At the end of summer 1980, they submitted proposals for course development.

A panel of women's studies scholars and disciplinary specialists was convened in September 1980 to review the course proposals. Three of the panelists, Elaine Marks (Women's Studies Research Center, University of Wisconsin-Madison), Lilli Hornig, and Roberta Ferron (Native American Studies, Montana State University), presented a seminar to critique the proposals and worked with individual faculty to strengthen their proposals. Faculty then revised their proposals, field-tested the courses, and submitted final reports on their work in May 1981.[2]

These reports highlighted course revision strategies, which fell generally into three categories: new courses focusing on women added to departmental offerings (e.g., Sex Differences in Speech Communication); new units or segments of material focusing on women or gender added to existing courses (e.g., a unit on Sexism and Language added to an English teaching methods course); and integration of new material on women throughout an existing course (e.g., History of Montana). In subsequent interviews with faculty, a number have reported that they were unsatisfied with the segregated unit approach and, as they have become more familiar with the material, have moved toward a fully integrated approach to teaching about women.

Project participation also resulted in measured changes in the faculty participants themselves.[3] A pre-test/post-test comparison group design using the short form of the Attitude Toward Women Scale[4] was employed to measure faculty attitude change. Analysis of results indicates that the WEEA Project had the effect of broadening participants' attitudes concerning the rights and roles of women in contemporary society. This result is striking, given the fact that, as a self-selected group, the project faculty were more liberal to begin with in their attitudes toward women than the randomly selected control group of their peers.

Attitude changes affected teaching behaviors. Faculty were asked in exit interviews if, as a result of the project participation, they had deliberately modified their classroom behaviors.[5] Only three out of the thirty-six interviewed reported no change. Common changes reported include: (1) modification of language style to avoid linguistic bias; (2) greater attention to nontraditional students in classroom discussions; (3) concerted efforts to place equal demands and expectations on all students; and (4) attempts to modify traditional hierarchical structures in the classroom.

Faculty were also queried about the impact of the project on their professional lives. The most frequently mentioned positive impact was that project involvement had allowed them more time for research and thus many had written, presented, or published papers on women and gender. Six faculty members reported dramatic changes in their research emphasis and planned to specialize in research on women or gender. Many also felt that their courses were better as a result of the project.

Lack of interest and support of departmental colleagues was the most commonly reported negative professional impact associated with the project. In some cases, faculty described their departmental colleagues as actively hostile to or derisive of their new research interest. Some felt that the project was viewed as "low-reward, service activity," and that they were at risk professionally for having participated.

In this project faculty had experiences similar to those reported by women's studies faculty elsewhere.[6] Their research interests allied them more closely with other project participants than with departmental colleagues who feel little obligation to teach about women in their courses. Many faculty participants felt that the potential for impact on the entire departmental curriculum through the curriculum review and planning process was greatest in those departments that had more than one participant and hence where an internal colleague-support system emerged.

Subsequent surveys of project participants indicate that they continue to review and revise courses to integrate the study of women. Many have consulted on campuses in the region, published articles, or given major presentations at national and regional meetings. In 1981, MSU hired a tenure-track specialist in United States women's history, due largely to the advocacy of a faculty member who participated in the project and who wanted a colleague in his own department with whom to discuss and collaborate on research. Since that time, three new courses focusing on women have been added to the department's curriculum. In the spring of 1984, an Introduction to Women's Studies was offered for the first time as a special topics course in sociology. Hence, the project also had the effect of expanding offerings in women's studies at Montana State University.

THE NORTHERN ROCKIES PROGRAM ON WOMEN IN THE CURRICULUM

The results of the MSU WEEA Project demonstrate that, with ample resources, one can significantly alter the teaching behaviors and research priorities of individual faculty members. Critical questions remained at the end of the project, however, such as:

- How much change is possible without large amounts of external funding?
- What is realistic to attempt internally in an era of shrinking resources and retrenchment?
- What are the key components necessary to a successful faculty development effort?

The opportunity to address these questions came when Montana State University received a two-year grant from the Fund for the Improvement of Postsecondary Education to assist other institutions in the region in initiating similar projects.

The Northern Rockies Program on Women in the Curriculum responded to specific regional needs. In its four-state area of Idaho, Montana, Utah, and Wyoming there are only five women's studies programs; only one, at the University of Utah, offers a baccalaureate degree in women's studies.

The economic climate in several of the states did not appear conducive to fostering the development of major new women's studies programs. On several campuses where such efforts had been attempted earlier, battle lines over the issue were drawn, and courses in women's studies currently operate out of women's centers rather than academic departments. The paucity of women's studies faculty and the distance to the nearest large center of feminist research, the University of Washington, argued for the development of more expertise on individual campuses and the creation of a means of interinstitutional exchange among neighboring schools. It was felt that a regional program would lend visibility to those programs in existence and enable other campuses to gain ideas and resources for program development.

To operate effectively on a small budget, the Northern Rockies Program on Women in the Curriculum built upon existing regional and institutional resources. It was cosponsored by the Northern Rockies Consortium for Higher Education (NORCHE), an established consortium of twenty-five schools that shares resources and consultants in faculty and curriculum development. NORCHE offered both an existing network of administrators and faculty interested in curricular innovation and a means of disseminating information on the new program through conferences and newsletters.

In contrast to the relatively generous support available to each individual faculty member who participated in the MSU Project (a total of $3,000), the financial assistance offered for institutional participation in the Northern Rockies Program was slim: a $2,000 stipend to apply to project activities and travel expenses for institutional representatives to attend two Program meetings. However, the Northern Rockies Program also made the experience and resources of the Montana State University Project available to participants and *attempted to substitute external validation and expertise for external funding.* Program participation included the opportunity to attend a four-day Institute on Women in the Curriculum held at MSU in April 1982, which was limited to Northern Rockies Program participants; a notebook of resources; access to a network of individuals working on similar projects; and technical assistance from the MSU Project staff throughout the two-year life of the Program.

Just as in the original WEEA Project, a call for proposals was used to generate interest in the Program. Application materials were sent to the chief academic officer at each of the fifty-one institutions in the four-state area with a liberal arts curriculum and an enrollment of at least one hundred students. A letter of introduction cosigned by the Program Director and a state representative from the Program Advisory Board accompanied these materials. In addition, brochures describing the Program were mailed to over 1,200 faculty and administrators in the region.

Support from NORCHE was critical in generating interest in the Program among administrators. The Program Advisory Board was composed of a president of one of the tribally controlled American Indian colleges in Montana, and several chief academic officers active in NORCHE, who contacted their colleagues throughout the region to explain the goals of the Program and urge their support. As a result, three chief academic officers, four deans, and seven department heads served on institutional teams and attended the Program Institute. Members of the Northwest Women's Studies Association also identified women's studies faculty and administrators to serve on institutional teams and as consultants to local projects.

Proposal guidelines asked applicants to describe local need and availability of resources for integrating women's studies into the curriculum and to identify a team responsible for project implementation. These teams had to include an academic administrator, with resources for faculty or curriculum development to commit to the local project, and faculty with expertise in women's studies and curriculum development. This approach was used expressly to establish ties between existing institutional programs dedicated to curricular change and faculty interested in the integration of women's studies into the curriculum.

Applications were received from twenty-two institutions. From this pool, ten project proposals were selected on the basis of quality, clarity, feasibility, and institutional commitment.

Program participants were all public, state-supported institutions and included the Universities of Idaho, Montana, Wyoming, and Utah; three state colleges; two of the seven community colleges in the Wyoming system; and the Montana College of Mineral Science and Technology. Central Wyoming College was the smallest, with an enrollment of approximately 550 students, and the University of Utah the largest, with 22,000 students. Three of the five institutions with women's studies programs were among those selected. The University of Utah program, initiated in 1974, offers a baccalaureate degree through the College of Social and Behavioral Sciences; the University of Wyoming, a minor in women's studies established in 1982; and Weber State College (Utah), a cluster of women's studies courses. Three of the institutions selected that do not have women's studies programs do have women's centers: the University of Idaho, the University of Montana, and Western Wyoming College. The centers at Idaho and Montana offer courses in women's studies and sponsored the annual conferences of the Northwest Women's Studies Association in 1981 and 1982 respectively. The University of Idaho project was written in conjunction with the Women's Studies Program at Washington State University.

These institutions experimented with diverse approaches to curricular change. The projects at the University of Wyoming, Western Wyoming College, and Lewis-Clark State College (Idaho) aimed at reform of courses fulfilling general education or departmental major requirements. Projects at Central Wyoming and Southern Utah State College conducted faculty development seminars and assisted faculty in the review and reform of regularly taught courses. The University of Utah developed a mentoring model for faculty development in women's studies. The projects at the University of Idaho/Washington State University and the University of Montana created networks of faculty to work on specific areas of curricular reform. Weber State College and Montana Tech designed projects to increase the participation and success of women in science and engineering respectively.

The Regional Program was administered by a small staff at Montana State University: a quarter-time Program director, a half-time Program coordinator, and a half-time administrative assistant. This staff, along with the local and regional advisory boards, provided assistance to the local projects. Formal Program activities in addition to the four-day training institute included a follow-up meeting held in conjunction with the annual meeting of the Northwest Women's Studies Meeting in October 1982 in Missoula, Montana; site visits by the Program director during the 1982–83 academic year; and a project evaluation conference held at the University of Utah in May 1983.

The support network created through the energies of the Program staff and participants enabled projects to accomplish more in a relatively short period of time than they might have through isolated or localized efforts. Program meetings allowed project representatives to share experiences, learn about progress at other institutions, identify resources, and discuss substantive issues in curricular reform. Their experiences are the basis for the practical approaches to project management contained in the following sections.

NOTES
1. Data collected and analyzed from the Northern Rockies Program on Women in the Curriculum include: (1) final reports submitted by the ten participating projects; (2) exit interviews conducted by an external evaluator with project directors or designees; (3) site visits by the author to participating campuses; and (4) reports from participants, consultants, and the external evaluator of three project meetings for institutional representatives. Data from the earlier Montana State University WEEA project include: (1) pre- and post-program survey of faculty attitudes toward women; (2) exit interviews with participating faculty; (3) a post-program survey of student attitudes; and (4) peer review of faculty proposals for course revision. See Schmitz and Williams, "Seeking Women's Equity through Curricular Reform," #60.
2. Faculty essays were edited and compiled into five books by project staff and submitted to the WEEA Publishing Center in August 1981; the manuscripts were approved for publication, but cutbacks in federal funds to the program have delayed production.
3. Anne S. Williams and Betty Schmitz, "Seeking Women's Equity

through Curricular Reform: Impact on Faculty and Student Participants" (Unpublished paper, Bozeman: Montana State University, 1982).

4. Janet T. Spence and Robert L. Helmreich, "The Attitude Toward Women Scale: An Objective Instrument to Measure Attitudes Toward the Rights and Roles of Women in Contemporary Society," *Journal Supplement Abstract Service Catalog of Selected Documents in Psychology* 2 (1972): 66.

5. See Schmitz and Williams, "Seeking Women's Equity through Curricular Reform," #60.

6. See Howe, *Seven Years Later*, #73, and "Feminist Scholarship," #8.

2

Designing a Project

Projects to incorporate the new scholarship on women into the traditional curriculum are faculty development projects. Substantive curricular change depends almost entirely on re-educating the hearts and minds of the faculty. Projects with the goals of transforming the curriculum must establish a program of systematic, long-term faculty development that takes into account the stages faculty experience in thinking about women. Those projects that have been the most successful in effecting curricular change have been those that have sustained faculty over a two- or three-year period through a series of seminars on feminist theory. A single faculty development workshop, with brief review of reading lists and syllabi, will, at best, result only in the addition of a token unit on women in an otherwise un-reconstructed course.

Curriculum change projects ultimately have to involve large numbers of faculty, both junior faculty who staff introductory courses that reach a large number of students and the senior faculty who control the shape of departmental and core curricula. Re-educating faculty to take feminist research and women seriously is no easy task. The success of this kind of project therefore depends foremost on the existence of permanent faculty with expertise in women's studies, strong administrative support for the project, the availability of resources, and an opportunity for faculty development.

Given these conditions, the first step in translating women's studies' long-term, radical vision of transforming the curriculum into an action agenda for a campus or consortial project is to set goals that take into account the individual characteristics of the institution, its history and current political climate, local needs, and the available human and financial resources that can be dedicated to the project.

ASSESSING THE CLIMATE FOR CHANGE
No matter what kind of change or innovation is contemplated, deciding on project goals, objectives, and activities requires first of all a careful assessment of institutional climate for change. Such questions as the following should be answered:

- What is the particular character of this institution?
- What activities does it value and reward?

- What parts of the mission statement speak to this kind of change?
- What is the current political climate?
- Is there an institutional process underway that the faculty and administration feel is important and that can be a vehicle for this kind of change?
- What are the forces that will support change and those that will hinder it?

Further questions relating to the specific nature of a project to integrate women's studies into the curriculum should then be addressed:

- How will the fact that the project focuses on women affect its reception?
- What is the institution's prior history with women's programs?
- How has the institution responded to equity concerns in general? To affirmative action and Title IX?
- What women's studies resources are available on campus?
- What will be the project's relationship to other women's programs on campus and in the community?

Most of the projects participating in the Northern Rockies Program used the Program call for proposals as a means to justify surveys of content on women in the curriculum or assessments of institutional climate for women. For example, the project planners at Southern Utah State College administered the Spence and Helmreich Attitude Toward Women Scale to the entire faculty to gauge the level of potential support for the project. The University of Montana project team sent a questionnaire to all faculty asking about the extent of women-related materials in their courses. The results of these assessments were used both as documentation of need for project proposals and as an indicator of faculty awareness for project planning.

Several good instruments exist to assess institutional progress toward the attainment of sex equity. Readers are referred in particular to the questionnaire from *Everywoman's Guide to Colleges and Universities*, #91, and the *Institutional Self-Study Guide on Sex Equity* prepared by Karen Bogart et al., #88.

DECIDING ON FOCUS AND OBJECTIVES

Deciding on objectives is directly related to available resources. It is difficult, for example, to initiate change in a period of retrenchment. Faculty are less likely to welcome the occasion to experiment with innovation in the classroom when they are concerned about maintaining student enrollments. Limited resources and a general climate of demoralization over cutbacks in programs may make it extremely difficult to initiate a project to transform the curriculum unless there is already a mechanism in place for curricular review and reform, such as a review of general education requirements. In this context, it is useful to consider carefully all the areas of potential impact and choose the one with the greatest chance for initial success or the one with the greatest potential for measurable impact.

The priority objectives of the institutions participating in the Northern Rockies Program on Women in the Curriculum were determined in part by the Program application guidelines, which set certain parameters on the scope of projects. Each applicant had to design ''a plan for curricular change to improve the learning environment for women students.'' This plan could include designing new courses on women, revising existing courses to include material on women, or conducting faculty or student development programs that would result in specific curricular change.

In response to these general guidelines, project objectives fell into three basic categories:

- to integrate new scholarship on women into targeted areas of the curriculum;
- to expand educational options for women students;
- to support both curricular change and change in the educational environment.

Each of these priorities for change raises issues of strategy and target group that will have to be taken into account during the early planning stages of the project.

Projects designed to integrate women's studies into targeted courses or curricula were conceived as a means of increasing the visibility and effectiveness of women's studies on campus or increasing the presence of feminist scholarship within the traditional curriculum. Specific concerns mentioned in these project proposals included: (1) the continuing omission of the study of women from standard courses; (2) bias in curricular materials; (3) an increased female enrollment, including older, returning women, who require a curriculum relevant to their lives; and (4) outdated, outmoded curricula that have not been revised in light of the tremendous growth of scholarship on women and gender.

Projects to expand educational options for women students in nontraditional areas also identified needs related to increased enrollments of women students. Research and statistics were gathered to demonstrate sex segregation in choice of majors, lack of female role models for women students, and bias in advising and curricular materials. Activities in this kind of project were two-fold: (1) those designed to treat the problem of bias against women by changing faculty attitudes and behaviors; and (2) those designed to assist the students themselves in recognizing and coping with bias. One problem to avoid in this type of project is the desire on the part of some faculty, when confronted with bias in their disciplines, to transfer the blame to textbooks, high school teachers, future employers, or to the student herself. Getting faculty to admit to the bias inherent in the structure of the disciplines and the university is a very difficult task, and many will look for a solution that does not entail personal self-examination.

Projects with multiple goals usually began as a loose coalition of people from various offices or programs in the institution who had identified specific needs in their own areas. These projects identified a combination of goals responding to the need to improve the quality of life for women students, raise the awareness of faculty to bias in the curriculum and in the education environment, create new courses on women and courses that incorporate the study of women, and improve recruitment and hiring patterns for women faculty and staff. Projects with multiple goals usually chose more general titles for the project, such as "Women in the Curriculum." The initial problem to be addressed in these projects was the sequencing of goals and the solicitation of agreement on the part of the various constituencies as to long-term and short-term project goals.

HAZARDS IN GOAL SETTING

Don't:

- confuse long-term and short-term goals.
- set goals that are too ambitious or too abstract.
- equate the entire effort with an externally funded program.
- try to do too much too fast.
- dilute the message of feminism!

Successful project leaders differentiated long-term goals, such as transforming the core curriculum through the incorporation of feminist scholarship, from short-term objectives, such as introducing faculty in specific departments to the new scholarship on women in their disciplines or establishing a computerized data base for accessing women's studies resources in campus libraries. Project leaders were careful not to set short-term goals that were too abstract or too ambitious, given the resources of the project; often they deliberately selected some short-term objectives that were immediately achievable to lay the groundwork for longer-term, more fundamental change and to provide some initial concrete rewards to the project leaders and participants.

It is important, however, not to set short-term, "manageable" goals with no longer-term vision. Once such immediate goals have been met, faculty and administrators may assume the project is over, even though no fundamental change has occurred. At the same time, it is a particular handicap to equate the long-term goals with a formal project, funded externally for a shorter period of time. Project leaders should plan from the outset to institutionalize their efforts in tangible ways that are clear and visible to both current and future participants. Revising policy or mission statements, designating funds for faculty development, and rewriting job descriptions with assigned responsibilities for curriculum integration efforts are some of the ways this can be done.

Another hazard in goal setting is the tendency to avoid controversial topics or issues in an attempt to win broad-based faculty support for the project. In general, projects that presented in-depth feminist analyses of middle-class, white, male bias in the structure and content of the academic disciplines and in power structures within the institution, and raised critical and challenging issues, were the most successful in engaging faculty in discussions that led to fruitful reform. The University of Wyoming project team, for example, invited biologist Ruth Hubbard of Harvard University as a keynote speaker on bias in science precisely because science is perceived as objective. In her after-dinner lecture Hubbard chose to underscore her message with examples from cross-cultural studies of menstruation. In the faculty workshop at Southern Utah State College, located in the predominantly Mormon community of Cedar City, Lynda Sexson of Montana State University spoke about patriarchal images of women in religion. Speaking the unspeakable is a component of disrupting the patriarchy. The anger or disbelief that surfaces when faculty are forced to confront bias as a systematic, pervasive problem is the necessary first stage in the change process.

Faculty coming to terms with feminism will do so in stages (see page 26). It is therefore best to present the full message from the start, from which they can select what they are willing to begin with, intellectually and personally. Presenting a watered-down message will only result in further dilution and the risk of not stimulating faculty to engage in the intellectual debate necessary for change. Besides, considerations of standards and intellectual honesty aside, it is difficult to predict what topics will offend faculty. In one instance, what appeared to project planners to be a rather innocuous workshop on forms of bias in curricular materials ended in an unpleasant shouting match between faculty and the outside consultant.

In a few cases, project leaders attempted to achieve too much change within the timeline of the externally funded project and, as a result, became discouraged, disappointed, or "burned out." The project timeline should balance available resources with goals for change and recognize that fundamental change is a long-term process.

Initial discussion of project goals should include discussion of what success would look like. How do we know when gender balance in the curriculum has been achieved? How is this balance related to the treatment of people of differing race, culture, class, or sexual identity? How will revised courses be judged? How will we know that faculty have improved their advising of women students? Questions like these will assist project planners in defining long- and short-term goals, and in focusing on collecting data that can be used for planning the implementation of longer-term goals and new projects.

PHASES OF CURRICULAR CHANGE

Peggy McIntosh has identified five interactive phases of curricular change that faculty experience in attempting to incorporate the study of women into their disciplines.[1] Using history as an example, she describes these phases as follows:

> *Phase 1:* Womanless History;
> *Phase 2:* Women in History;
> *Phase 3:* Women as a Problem, Anomaly, or Absence in History;
> *Phase 4:* Women *as* History;
> *Phase 5:* History Reconstructed, Redefined, and Transformed to
>   include us all.

In Phase 1 thinking, the absence of women from the discipline is not noted and the curriculum is perceived as true and objective in its representation of the best that has been done and thought. In Phase 2, a place is made in the syllabus for a few women who have made it by traditional standards. This is the phase in which one talks about the "unique contributions of women" to a specific discipline. McIntosh compares this phase to a kind of affirmative action program. It assumes that the disciplines, like the institution, are functioning well and that all the "have-not's" could possibly want is a higher slot on the reading list or in the system. In Phase 3, we begin to understand the politics of a curriculum that has systematically excluded not only women, but most of the world's population, in fact, everyone who is not white, upper-middle class, and male. In this phase, one gets angry at classifications that characterize women as an anomaly or problem and begins to challenge the assumptions underlying the disciplines that result in such labeling.

In Phase 4, thinking becomes transformative. Curriculum work in this phase involves asking different research questions designed to elucidate what women's experience really was and is. It is also the phase in which the boundaries between the disciplines break down as answers to these new questions come from throughout existing bodies of knowledge. Phase 5, ideally, would involve piecing all the knowledge back together again to produce a new view of the whole.

In effect, all faculty must pass through these phases as curricular change work is undertaken, and the amount of time it will take a given individual to reach Phase 4 is not predictable. Resources must be available to support faculty as they move beyond Phases 2 and 3, begin to develop a radical vision of an inclusive curriculum and seek opportunities for interdisciplinary work. The large, externally funded curriculum integration projects were able to support selected groups of faculty over a two- to three-year period. However, models exist to show that significant change in faculty research and teaching priorities can occur without large amounts of external funding.

Guilford College (North Carolina) has been encouraging the integration of women's studies for nearly a decade without an external grant. Efforts toward such curriculum integration have been made possible through an internal program for faculty development that has provided funds to sponsor outside speakers, discussion groups, films, and retreats. These activities provided a forum for faculty to discuss deficiencies in the curriculum and ways of incorporating women's studies research into standard courses. Carol Stoneburner, Coordinator of Women's Studies and Director of Faculty Development, has seen such activities lead to specific course and curricular revisions and believes that faculty study groups that sustain faculty interest over a period of time are particularly effective.[2] Interdisciplinary research and curriculum design groups organized around a specific topic and cluster of courses is also the model for change used by Smith College.

The University of Idaho/Washington State University project is another example of this approach. The major objective of this project was to create a network of scholars and teachers at both institutions and in the community who would work to achieve change both collectively and individually. Seven interdisciplinary faculty task forces were created to design faculty development activities in a variety of disciplines. The $2,000 from the Northern Rockies Program served as seed money to launch initial efforts and as a resource for grant development. The project was conceived from the outset as one of long-term faculty development to be sustained by the commitment and interest of those who participate in the initial activities (see page 84).

Once faculty become engaged with feminist theory and begin to do research and writing on women and gender, they begin to take advantage of other resources to sustain their intellectual growth: internal faculty development funds for research or instructional improvement, opportunities to teach in interdisciplinary programs, speakers' or visiting scholars' funds to bring a feminist scholar to their department or college, and seminars or panels on women's studies at professional association meetings. The project, in effect, becomes institutionalized among the faculty members themselves, who become committed to feminist theory as a means for personal and institutional transformation.

STRUCTURAL MODELS FOR REFORM

Marilyn Schuster and Susan Van Dyne, in their survey of current projects to transform the curriculum,[3] identify three structural models for reform, each with inherent advantages and disadvantages:

1. A top-down model begun with an administrative directive to make sweeping changes in the curriculum by integrating introductory courses in all departments or otherwise affecting a significant number of basic courses.
2. A piggy-back model in which interdisciplinary courses or programs already sanctioned within the institutional agenda are targeted as the best way to begin curriculum transformation and to reach a broad range of faculty.
3. A bottom-up coordination or consortial model that originates with faculty and seeks to highlight, connect, and maximize internal resources and to do faculty outreach.

Projects in the Northern Rockies Program are exemplary of these approaches. The "top-down" model describes projects at Western Wyoming College, Montana Tech, and Lewis-Clark State College (Idaho), initiated through the presence of an academic administrator on the project team who wanted to encourage and support major revisions in specific areas of the curriculum. At Montana Tech, for example, the project responded to an institutional mandate to increase the enrollment of women students in the engineering curriculum.

The advantages of this model are obvious in that the project has the sanction and resources of the administration. Faculty are more likely to espouse innovation if they feel it is viewed positively by administrators and that they will be rewarded professionally for participating. This model works best in institutions where faculty are accustomed to taking direction in curricular matters from academic administrators or in periods of institutional change. It has an obvious disadvantage: the top-down model is likely to generate resistance in faculty who feel that curricular matters are within their own purview. Thus, in projects initiated by administrators, a strategy is needed to minimize faculty resistance.

Projects at Southern Utah State College and the University of Wyoming used the "piggy-back" model, were identifying an existing program or process through which they could achieve their goals. Both institutions were in the early stages of major curricular review processes when the call for proposals from the Northern Rockies Program was sent out. It appeared advantageous to the project planners to use Program resources to increase their ability to influence the direction of these curricular reviews. The Wyoming project offered a means through which the Women's Studies Committee and the General Education Committee could work together to develop a process to review courses proposed for the new general education requirements for content on women and minorities. The Southern Utah project provided women's studies resources to faculty who received Title III grants for the review and reform of their courses.

The advantage of this model is that, if successful, the impact will be felt at the heart of the institution. Projects that use existing programs or priorities also do not require as many resources, since they are built upon existing committees or other organizational structures. The disadvantage is that project leaders do not control the reward structure and hence must work through persuasion rather than mandate. There is also the danger, as Schuster and Van Dyne point out, that the revision of one area of the curriculum will swallow up the entire project effort.

The majority of the projects, however, used a "bottom-up" approach, as might be expected from the structure of the Northern Rockies Program itself and more generally from the history of campus activity in women's studies in the region. Minimal external resources were available and, in order to increase the potential for impact on the curriculum, had to be matched by capitalizing on internal resources. Through coalition building and outreach efforts, networks of individuals from across campus were identified to share resources and plan strategies for change. This model was used in the joint University of Idaho/Washington State University project mentioned earlier and in the Weber State Project, which brought together academic faculty with counseling staff, consultants from the Sex Desegregation Assistance Center, and the Utah Math/Science Network to design a program to expand options for women in nontraditional fields at both the secondary and postsecondary levels.

One advantage of this approach is that it brings together people from throughout the institution who can share information and design change strategies with greater knowledge of the total system. However, it is riddled with the problems of any coalition or consortium: the primary commitment of those involved will always be to their own program or agenda first, and if they do not perceive the benefit of project goals to this agenda, or if they disagree on the strategies decided upon, they will tend to become disenchanted. There is also the danger that the radical agenda will be lost at the outset in an effort to build broad-ranging support.

Structural models were also shown to have influenced decisions about the target audience for project activities. Projects operating with strong administrative support or institutional mandate were able to target all faculty in specific departments and attempt integration of the study of women into specific courses or curricula. All faculty within the targeted department participated in seminars, were provided with resources, and were expected to revise their courses. Projects using the piggy-back or consortial model tended either to work from the out-set with the "already committed," or to conduct an all-faculty semi-nar or retreat, followed by solicitation of a core group to participate in further seminars or receive support for course revision. Some projects began with plans to influence an entire department or pro-gram, but meeting with resistance and not having enough adminis-trative support, modified their plans and worked with those faculty who expressed interest.

NOTES
1. "Interactive Phases of Curricular Re-Vision," in Spanier et al., #62, pp. 25–34; and #45.
2. "Guilford College," *Forum for Liberal Education* 4, 1 (October 1981): 11–12.
3. "Project on Women and Social Change: Smith College," in Spanier et al., #62, pp. 59–72. See also #61.

3

Initiating the Project

CHOOSING AN ADMINISTRATIVE LOCATION AND PROJECT LEADERS

Thorough knowledge of the power structure of the institution will allow careful assessment of the benefits and costs of alternative administrative locations for a curriculum integration project. Of the ten projects participating in the Northern Rockies Program, three were located in the office of the vice president for academic affairs or academic dean, three in the department to be targeted by the reform, two within women's studies programs, one in student services, and one in continuing education. The choice of these locations depended on several factors: the approach, the target audience, and the commitment of key individuals. In some cases, project leaders acknowledged that the choice of location was not ideal, but had been made because of the amount of support a particular office could offer to the project.

The most successful projects were those placed within established programs or offices, particularly high priority ones, and were directed by persons who reported directly to (or had access to) the dean or department head with authority over areas of the curriculum to be affected. In most cases, this administrator had attended the initial program institute and was supportive of change. The commitment of these administrators had been carefully assessed prior to implementing the project. Evidence of this commitment translated into matching funds, "mandates," or strong suggestions to faculty to participate in the program, and merit points that resulted in salary increments. It is important, however, that the project not depend on the sole support of one administrator, since changes in administrators or their responsibilities are frequent. A wide base of support must be developed so that the project can survive reorganizations and personnel changes. As an example, in the course of the first year of one project, there were three different deans and two different presidents.

The selection of the project director or project leaders parallels issues of placement. Projects with goals to change profoundly the method and content of the curriculum must target senior faculty. Project leaders who occupy strategic positions in the power structure of the university or college have a better chance of influencing this group. The director should ideally be someone who possesses leadership ability, who commands the respect of peers and who is committed to over-

31

seeing the effort for some established period of time. Choosing some-one who is respected as a scholar/teacher but who has not been actively involved in women's advocacy on campus may be advanta-geous in developing new leadership; support from others with exper-tise in women's studies will be essential, however.

Issues of project leadership raise parallel concerns related to the status of women in higher education and make it clear that curricular change must go hand in hand with hiring and tenuring women faculty and faculty committed to feminist teaching and research. In general, those who are interested in and committed to the goals of integrating the study of women into the curriculum and who are the most knowledgeable about the new scholarship on women are the younger, untenured faculty women, or women in part-time or temporary posi-tions. Participation in such a project may be a risky endeavor for these women as they work toward tenure or toward a permanent position within the institution. On the other hand, if the project is a visible and important one to the institution, one that key administrators and faculty want to see work, it may represent an opportunity to demon-strate one's talent in managing a change process. Such projects do af-ford visibility and an opportunity to test one's mettle, often more than one would like! They also present an opportunity to acquire a full range of management skills for future administrative positions.

The Northern Rockies Program avoided some of the issues of pro-ject leadership by requiring the involvement of a team of individuals including an administrator and faculty with expertise in women's studies and curriculum development. Most project planners ensured that the team included someone who could lead the faculty (even if only in a symbolic way), someone who could provide resources, and someone who knew what had to be done and how to get it done.

Several projects participating in the Northern Rockies Program in-cluded a member of the library staff on the project team or advisory board. Librarians were able to assist in a number of ways: identifying resources for faculty projects; preparing special bibliographies of library holdings in women's studies; or allocating funds at their disposal to purchase new holdings in women's studies.

OBTAINING INSTITUTIONAL COMMITMENT

Early in the planning stages, project leaders should assess the interest and commitment of all those with a stake in the project and those who can provide human or financial resources. Consulting key actors in the system and allowing them to contribute ideas to the design of the pro-ject helps them to "buy into" the project at some level and ensures that they are informed about project goals, even if they adopt a wait-and-see attitude or offer only tacit approval. Commitment from administrators should come in some tangible form: matching funds, travel funds, merit points for project participation, released time for project leaders, and so forth.

The Northern Rockies Program on Women in the Curriculum offered participating institutions $2,000 in seed money for 1982-83. The total budgets for the projects as reported in their final reports (excluding the released time or donated time of the project directors) averaged about $4,800 and ranged up to, in one case, over $10,000. This is evidence of the project leaders' ability to garner institutional support to initiate project activities. One factor that contributed to their ability to negotiate was the external validity accorded local projects through the NORCHE sponsorship of the Program. NORCHE Board members not only endorsed the Program; they served as members of the Advisory Board and encouraged colleagues to lend support to project proposals that emerged on their campuses.

There are a number of other ways administrators can help, and did so in these projects:

- Providing "maps" to the institutional power structure and facilitating the right connections for project leaders;
- Reinterpreting the institutional or departmental mission to encourage curricular reform to incorporate the study of women and minorities;
- Attending project functions and giving public recognition to reform efforts;
- Rewarding those doing feminist work; appointing feminists to key committees and task forces;
- Asking for studies or surveys that document problems that the project is addressing.

The most effective administrators were those who saw to it that the curricular reform efforts were initiated and directed by faculty while offering the requisite moral, financial, and political support.

Caveat: Test the "ownership" and commitment of the key individuals before a public activity. If they have only bought into the project on a superficial level, or because they have been persuaded against their better judgment, they may not support the project when the going gets rough. Their own knowledge of the issues and conception of the importance of the project may falter when challenged by colleagues. On occasion, women project leaders were deserted by higher-level administrators and faculty on the project team in the face of general faculty resistance at a seminar, or found themselves the only ones willing to be identified with a project that had become controversial.

WORKING WITH AN ADVISORY BOARD

The majority of projects, including the host Program at Montana State University, used advisory boards to develop the support and visibility necessary for a successful project. These boards were generally of two types: small, working committees of knowledgeable and committed individuals who generated, implemented, evaluated and, where necessary, modified project activities; and broadly based boards of a more diverse nature and more representative of both the power structure and the target area, who acted as sounding boards for project plans and suggested ways of achieving project objectives. Selection of members of advisory boards was based on a number of criteria: representation from disciplines or units of the institution, representation from women and cultural minorities, persons respected by their peers within the institution, persons knowledgeable about the power structure of the institution and able to get things done. In some cases, these criteria resulted in the choice of persons not fully sensitized to nor supportive of women's issues, but whose eventual support was deemed critical. In such cases, it is essential to allow time for the board to work through its own resistance.

The Montana State University Project on Women in the Curriculum, which oversaw the development and implementation of the Northern Rockies Program, provides an illustration of effective ways to use advisory boards. Because of the number and scope of project activities and outcomes, which included the production of a sourcebook on integrating the study of women into the curriculum (see # 57) as well as provision of support to campus projects, three separate boards with different functions were set up: a national review board to oversee the development of project materials; a regional advisory board to assist in the recruitment of project participants; and a local advisory committee to select project participants and advise on project implementation.

Members of the local advisory committee were selected to represent diverse academic areas, complementary areas of expertise, and commitment to project goals. The regional board was selected on the basis of members' leadership ability and influence, and to represent diverse types of institutions and the different states and populations within the region. The national board was composed of women's studies scholars active in curriculum integration efforts. The primary criterion for selection of members on all three boards was, however, their willingness to make a commitment of their time and energy to the project.

All three boards were kept purposely small and focused on the tasks to be accomplished. These were outlined at the outset with an estimate of the amount of time board activities would entail. Interaction with the national board was handled through correspondence; the regional board convened at meetings of the Northern Rockies Consortium for Higher Education; and the local committee met once a month in the first year of the project and quarterly during the second year. Members of the local committee were informed well in advance of meetings and also sent the materials and agenda items that would be discussed. At the beginning of each meeting, the board was informed of how their recommendations had been implemented so they could see in concrete fashion the results of their deliberations and suggestions. Board members also appreciate more visible involvement and rewards, such as being asked to introduce speakers at program activities and receiving letters acknowledging their individual contributions to project success, with copies to appropriate administrators.

CAPITALIZING ON EXISTING INSTITUTIONAL AGENDAS

It is more effective in seeking institutional support for a project to show an administrator how the goals of the project, if accomplished, will help solve a problem or issue already acknowledged as an institutional priority rather than seeking to add another priority to an already long list. There may be an institutional process underway that can be furthered or improved by a joint effort. Or, it may be possible to demonstrate that attention to women in the curriculum or support of faculty development in women's studies can help to alleviate some pressing institutional problem.

Project leaders were creative in using current campus concerns to the benefit of their own goals. These included: accreditation reviews; institutional goals for affirmative action; goals for increased enrollments in specific areas; general education reviews; redefinition of the institutional mission in relation to the liberal arts and professions; or concern for the quality of teaching and scholarship.

Integrating women's studies into the curriculum offers support to these kinds of institutional priorities in explicit ways. For coeducational institutions that are experiencing shifts in enrollment patterns, developing a curriculum that reflects the experience of all students and provides a more accurate portrayal of social reality is critical to attracting and retaining students. Alleviating bias against women and cultural minorities in nontraditional disciplines and improving the advising process can be crucial factors in student retention. Projects to integrate women's studies into the curriculum can provide a vehicle for a thorough review and critique of a college or departmental curriculum to see if it is meeting the needs of students. The interdisciplinary networks for research and teaching that develop from these kinds of projects can offer renewed intellectual stimulation to faculty that results in improved teaching and increased faculty publication. These arguments may be convincing to administrators seeking to improve the academic standing of an institution.

With the growth and development on a national scale of projects to integrate the new scholarship on women, especially into liberal arts curricula, it is easier to show that an institution is not keeping up with the times and offering an out-of-date, outmoded curriculum. This was one critical role of the regional effort represented in the Northern Rockies Program: to point to the efforts underway at peer institutions in an attempt to get something started at home. An inexpensive position paper is available from the Association of American College's Project on the Status and Education of Women that can be distributed to administrators and faculty as an argument for innovation (see #50). A series of discipline-specific critiques have been produced by scholars participating in the New England Faculty Development Project at the Wellesley College Center for Research on Women (##23, 32, 35, 38, 39, 64, 108).

Sometimes a simple appeal to the unbiased pursuit of the truth or to the philosophical principle of equality, delivered by an eloquent speaker, can be convincing. Examples of speeches from seminars and conferences on the new scholarship on women and its potential for transforming the disciplines are found in the bibliography, ##28, 41, 42, 45, 51–54, 62, 63.

ELICITING FACULTY PARTICIPATION
Deciding Whom to Involve
The ultimate success of any curricular reform project depends on the quality and commitment of the faculty involved in the effort. Curricular change that is initiated, developed, and evaluated by faculty members in response to their own critical assessment of the needs of students and the mission of the undergraduate curriculum has the greatest potential for impact.

To select incentives that will appeal to faculty, one must know where they are concerned intellectually and politically, and what sustains them in their work. Faculty do not respond to the same sorts of arguments for change that administrators do. They are wary of political agendas and resist reshaping curricula in response to what they view as fads. Faculty oriented toward teaching will respond to different incentives than those oriented toward research. Projects in institutions where the faculty and administration are at odds must be cautious of aligning themselves with programs or agendas faculty do not value, or with programs that may be transitory.

One of the key questions to decide early in planning is who can or who should change? Who is the project designed for? The entire faculty? A core group? Senior faculty? Those who are interested and sympathetic to project goals? Those who teach large, introductory courses? Those active in curricular change on campus? This decision, like that of who should lead the project, is linked to the political climate of the institution and the degree of sophistication of the faculty.

In their degree of awareness of feminist issues in relation for the curriculum, campuses in the Northern Rockies Program fell into three categories: 1) those with very few women's resources and little awareness among faculty about feminist scholarship, women's equity issues, or women's studies; 2) campuses with developed women's studies programs that offer a degree or provide a cluster of courses for students; and 3) those in between, with limited resources, often in the form of a strong and visible women's center and some women's studies courses, but no formalized curriculum in women's studies and, in some cases, residual negative attitudes among faculty resulting from earlier efforts to establish a women's studies program. None of the participating campuses had initiated a formal project to integrate women's studies into the curriculum.

Campuses with few existing resources in women's studies elected either to use project resources to build general faculty awareness and then solicit proposals for course revision from a core of interested persons, or to target specific departments and concentrate resources in one area that could become a model for change for the general faculty. Women's studies consultants were brought in to give major presentations and work with faculty on specific plans for curriculum reform. In most cases, faculty participation in these seminars was strongly urged by a dean or vice president.

The University of Wyoming project, operating out of a strong women's studies program and with the full support of the dean, also elected to target a specific group of faculty: the general education committee and the departmental representatives who would oversee the development of departmental courses being proposed to meet a new set of requirements. The potential for impact of women's studies scholarship on this central area of the curriculum was the key factor in this decision.

In targeting specific departments or areas of the curriculum, planners had to weigh a number of factors. In some cases, those departments offering large core courses required of all students were selected because of the potential number of students who would be exposed to the new material on women (see Western Wyoming College, pages 71-73). In other cases, departments experiencing large enrollment increases of women students, particularly older, returning adults, were selected (see Lewis-Clark State College, pages 73-75). No matter where one begins with faculty recruitment, if the larger goal of a transformed curriculum is to be attained, a large number of faculty from all disciplines will have to be brought into the effort.

Some project leaders wanted to avoid the "high profile" approach associated with the faculty seminars and inservice training until a new advocacy base for women's studies could be developed. This was the case both on campuses where women's studies was losing support and those where the battle lines were drawn over the place of women's studies in the curriculum. Project leaders adopted the short-term goal of developing networks among feminist faculty—both female and male—and building a larger base of support from which to launch curricular reform efforts. Informal persuasion and the one-on-one approach was used to solicit the participation of key individuals. The University of Utah mentoring project and the University of Idaho/Washington State University task force approach are examples of projects that aimed to provide opportunities for development in women's studies to a core group of sympathetic faculty.

It is important to point out that avoiding a high profile may be next to impossible. In male-dominated institutions, the very fact of being a woman is high profile; by talking about women in positive terms and urging colleagues to accept a feminist vision, we become even more visible. And there will be those who attempt to punish us for it. Men who speak in support of feminism are not immune to scorn, and project leaders, male and female, should be secure in their own commitment to project goals and in their willingness to take risks for the sake of change.

Choosing Incentives

At a workship on integrating women's studies into the traditional curriculum, a women's studies director asked: "How much money do you have to pay faculty to get them to participate in a project like this? $200? $500? How much?" This question has several answers. All the projects surveyed for the 1981 SIROW report on *How to Integrate Women's Studies into the Curriculum* (#30) had attempted to enlist a balance of faculty from various disciplines on campus, including a high percentage of tenured faculty. These projects had, for the most part, large external grants that allowed project leaders to provide financial incentives in the form of stipends or released time (ranging from $200 to $10,000), travel funds, or book stipends to faculty participants. However, other incentives were also cited as effective: the promise of intellectual stimulation and interaction with colleagues, particularly on those campuses that are highly departmentalized; the opportunity to participate in a seminar series or special institute with outside consultants; and, in those projects aimed primarily at developing materials for a national audience, the promise of publication.

In one sense, becoming knowledgeable about the new scholarship on women and committed to its implications for curricular change is a matter of professional responsibility, not money. Most feminist scholars and teachers in academe have developed and revised courses on their own time, out of personal and professional commitment, without being paid to do so. Offering stipends or released time to the as-yet-unconverted, while asking these committed faculty to donate their time to the project, is obviously an inappropriate strategy.

It is worth noting that creating a sense of community and interest in curricular change among faculty will go a long way toward replacing dollars. Once faculty become intellectually excited by a question, they refocus their work, set new research priorities, and use means available to them through departmental or general funds to support their nascent interest. However, resources are needed to offer seminars and activities to capture their interest and to provide initial professional development opportunities. And, if the goal of the project is that of extensive, short-term change in individual faculty members or in extensive areas of the curriculum, and the requisite resources are available, stipends or released time for faculty participants is an effective strategy. The amount of money will depend on what is customary for the institution.

Projects participating in the Northern Rockies Program could not provide major financial incentives and hence had to rely on other forms of encouragement. In their final reports, project directors rated in priority order what they perceived to be the three most effective nonfinancial incentives for faculty: intellectual stimulation; the opportunity to work with outside consultants; and the opportunity to improve classroom teaching.

Also deemed important in eliciting faculty participation was the opportunity to work on an agenda that promised concrete, short-term results. At the University of Montana, for example, a new procedure that allows students to declare minors provided the impetus for a group of faculty to coalesce around the goals of expanding, coordinating, and making more visible to students women's studies offerings and presenting a proposal for allocation of a part-time permanent position for introductory and capstone women's studies courses to the university budget planning committee.

Strategies considered particularly effective for eliciting faculty participation included:

- Holding a special faculty workshop or seminar to discuss the new scholarship on women. This was done in some cases for selected departments on a regular inservice day, for selected faculty in a retreat setting, or for the entire faculty within the context of addressing issues of primary concern to the institution;
- Using a call for proposals mode to choose participants in order to allow faculty to define their own approach to curricular reform within their discipline or within specific courses;

- Providing consultant help in accomplishing an existing task or pressing departmental problem, such as preparing for an accreditation review, preparing departmental documents for program reviews, reviewing the core curriculum. Outside funds garnered for speakers or consultants can both assist with these agendas and introduce faculty to curricular concepts from women's studies;
- Providing resources and technical assistance in the form of bibliographies, course revision models, library search services, assistance in course design;
- Providing through project participation the opportunity for interdisciplinary work or team-teaching;
- Providing small stipends for acquisition of books or travel to professional meetings;
- Awarding merit or salary points for project participation;
- Conducting surveys of content on women in the curriculum or of faculty attitudes to document the existence of bias and justify the need for change.

Perceived intellectual content and quality of the program were essential in eliciting faculty participation. In publicizing faculty workshops, project leaders used language that invoked substantive issues in curricular reform. Seminars were designed around topics of intellectual interest to the faculty, and noted and respected speakers were chosen who could challenge the faculty with questions of substance.

Symbolic content was also important. The University of Idaho chose the theme "Missing Voices" for their seminar series and newsletter. An artist was commissioned to design a poster with faces of women and men, the women having no mouths. The theme hence provided both symbolic content for the issue and a pleasing way to identify the project and provide continuity among the various seminar topics and project activities.

Those campuses that elected to begin projects with a general faculty seminar were successful in creating a common experience from which to launch follow-up activities with specific faculty members. Even in those cases where the seminar was mandatory and there was some degree of hostility on the part of faculty, who either resented being told what to do or were completely unsympathetic to the topic, project leaders felt the strategy was a good one. It stirred up the faculty, created a common vocabulary for future change efforts, and documented the need for change. Some felt that the seminar was an ideal way of assessing the climate for change, in that it elicited unexpected stances, both for and against, on the part of the faculty. In cases where the seminars were mandatory, project leaders had already anticipated some degree of resistance and had discussed ways of handling it with the seminar consultants.

The projects at larger institutions selected multiple strategies, each of which was designed to appeal to a specific group of faculty. In the approach used by the University of Idaho/Washington State University project, the task forces each defined their own plan of action: the Task Force on Science and Technology put together a workshop series on classroom climate; the Humanities Task Force wrote a grant to conduct a major conference on curriculum revision in the humanities; the Social Sciences Task Force planned and sponsored a series of talks by Barrie Thorne. Each of these activities, tied together by the "Missing Voices" theme, was conceived as a means that would lead to further discussion about curricular revision in specific departments.

DESIGNING A FACULTY DEVELOPMENT SEMINAR

The lead-off activity for most projects to integrate women's studies into the curriculum is a faculty development seminar, usually with a well-known scholar/activist in women's studies who presents a rationale for transforming the curriculum and gives examples of the impact of feminist scholarship on the disciplines. (For information on consultants, see the Wellesley College Center for Research on Women's *Directory of Consultants*, #183; and Mairs et al., *Directory of Consultants in the West*, #184.) Since the success of future project activities aimed at course revision will depend to a large extent on the success of the seminar, it should be carefully planned in both structure and content.

The faculty seminars at the University of Wyoming and Southern Utah State College provide good examples of how to design and implement a successful faculty development workshop. These examples complement each other well, since the institutions and the projects represent very different settings and different approaches to the integration of women's studies into the curriculum.

The University of Wyoming has a Women's Studies Program offering a minor, and a dean of the College of Arts and Sciences who is very supportive of women's studies and who gave the program its initial mandate both to develop a strong curriculum in women's studies and to initiate efforts to incorporate feminist research into the main curriculum. The University has also had resources for both curriculum and faculty development. A review and restructuring of general education requirements in the College, combined with the availability of funds from the Northern Rockies Program, provided the impetus for initiating a project to fulfill the dean's second mandate. The project was designed to influence General Education Committee members and departmental representatives to review courses proposed for the new core for content on women and minorities.

Southern Utah State College was in a period of growth and change. A new president had been given a mandate to double and diversify the College's enrollment and build up the liberal arts program; a number of new faculty had been hired. In 1981, the College received a Title III grant to review and reform the curriculum. Through this grant, thirty-six faculty received support for reviewing curricula at comparable institutions and updating and revising courses. The College does not have a women's studies program, although a Women's Resource Committee has sponsored one course per term since 1976. The curriculum integration project was designed to offer resources and technical assistance to faculty who received Title III grants so that their course revisions would take women and minorities into account.

The faculty seminars at these two institutions targeted different groups of faculty. The Wyoming seminar, "Women's Studies and General Education: Combining Forces," was designed for a group of sixty people: the General Education Committee, the Women's Studies Committee, and the general education departmental representatives in the College of Arts and Sciences. It was preceded in 1980 by a series of speakers on general education, two of whom had addressed the need to incorporate women's and minority perspectives in the core curriculum. The Southern Utah State College workshop was held for the entire faculty and was the first required faculty development activity in five years.

Neither of the two faculty groups had been previously recruited to the project, and they were not offered any financial incentives for participation. Seminar planners thus had to devise strategies for attracting them to the seminar and capturing and sustaining their interest. These strategies included: an intellectually challenging set of seminar topics; a good balance of consultants and speakers; cosponsorship by representative groups; letters from appropriate administrators urging faculty participation; a balance of structured presentation, guided discussion, and unstructured social events at the seminar; and good timing and publicity.

Keynote topics chosen for the seminars addressed bias in research methods and teaching. At the Wyoming seminar, Ruth Hubbard dispelled the myth of scientific objectivity and at Cedar City, Lynda Sexson presented a critique of patriarchal bias in religion. In the latter instance, however, since the seminar was required of all Southern Utah State College faculty and since the campus environment is a more conservative one, considerable thought was placed into making sure the message would be heard. The seminar was titled "Academic Excellence through Curriculum Development," and a second keynote address on curriculum reform by the Dean of Liberal Education at University of Utah, a well-known and well-respected leader in the state, was scheduled. Faculty were then able to select from a number of concurrent follow-up sessions. Project leaders felt that those faculty who might be overtly hostile to the topic could choose to avoid the sessions on women's studies, thus making the small-group discussions more productive.

Project planners at the two institutions chose a balanced group of speakers for the seminars. There was a mixture of on-campus and off-campus consultants; representatives of different disciplines in the sciences and humanities; and people who could speak to the exclusion of racial and ethnic minorities from the curriculum in higher education. There was also a balance in seminar presentations of theory and practical application to specific disciplines and courses. Time was set aside for faculty to interact on an individual basis with the outside consultants and with colleagues from other disciplines. At the Wyoming seminar, one of these interactions resulted in a faculty member from computer science and one from art history planning a team-taught interdisciplinary course.

The Wyoming seminar was cosponsored by the Women's Studies Committee and the General Education Committee, and the Dean of Arts and Sciences wrote a letter to all faculty explaining her expectations for seminar participation and results. The project planning team at SUSC secured cosponsorship for their seminar internally from the Women's Resource Committee, the Faculty Development Task Force, and the Multicultural Center; and externally from the Northern Rockies Consortium for Higher Education and the Utah Association of Academic Professionals. The Academic Vice President sent out a letter of invitation to all faculty stressing the importance of the seminar for future curriculum planning at the institution.

Both seminars were held at the beginning of the academic year, before faculty became too busy with classes and committee assignments. Information about the topics and speakers was sent out well in advance to stimulate faculty interest. The Wyoming project team used additional strategies to encourage participation: the keynote address was scheduled as an after-dinner presentation and faculty spouses were invited to attend; the second day of the seminar was held at the University's mountain retreat. At SUSC, the first day of the seminar concluded with a cook-out at a college-owned cabin located in one of the nearby canyons. In this way opportunities were created at both seminars for interaction and discussion in less structured settings.

These are some of the components that went into designing successful seminars at these two institutions. Recommendations of things to do before, during, and after a seminar, based on these two examples, include:

Before the seminar...
Discuss seminar goals, organization, potential speakers, and

projected outcomes with a broadly based planning committee
or advisory board.

Inform and seek input from appropriate faculty committees and
administrators early in the planning process.

Seek out cosponsors for the event that will lend credibility.

Choose a topic that is of special interest to faculty and that
addresses current campus concerns.

Choose a time for the seminar that will ensure the maximum
participation of the targeted faculty group.

Send out information on the purpose and theme of the seminar well
in advance; include information on the speakers, perhaps
an article to read to stimulate interest.

Choose consultants who have a good reputation for presentations
on campuses similar to yours; write them about your
expectations and send them materials about the campus and
your project.

Choose speakers who can represent and present the experience and
perspectives of women of differing racial and ethnic backgrounds.

Develop an agenda that combines theory with practical application.

Choose a site and room arrangement that are conducive to
discussion and interaction.

Invite appropriate faculty and/or administrators to introduce
speakers.

Send out an agenda or reminder a week before the seminar.

Contact the press; offer an article relevant to the seminar
topic to the campus paper; arrange interviews if appropriate.

Prepare packets of relevant materials to distribute to faculty
at the seminar.

Prepare a questionnaire to evaluate the seminar.

During the seminar...

Briefly explain seminar schedule and state anticipated outcomes.

Keep session on schedule, but allow for discussion and questions.

Encourage discussion that moves from theory to application.

Be prepared to deviate from the agenda to meet needs or concerns
that arise.

Encourage individual interactions between outside speakers and
faculty.

Inform faculty of anticipated follow-up activities and what is
expected of them.

Ask consultants to write letters evaluating the seminar to
appropriate administrators or funding agencies.

Include time for evaluation or call attention to the evaluation
form in the packet and when and how it is to be completed.

After the seminar...
   Send out a letter to participants with the evaluation results or
     a follow-up article; inform them of future activities.
   Write thank-you letters to consultants; include evaluation results.
   Do a follow-up article for the campus newspaper.
   Hold a meeting of the advisory board to assess seminar results.
   Inform appropriate faculty groups and administrators of the
     seminar results; have someone do this for you who can
     praise your efforts and comment on their importance!

   Choice of topic may be one of the stumbling blocks for a project
planning team. With so much to choose from, where should one begin? In some cases the disciplines targeted by the project will determine the choice of topic; in others, the availability of a specific consultant. The University of Arizona experience with three years of
faculty development workshops in women's studies has yielded one
successful formula (see program below). For a group of faculty who
have already committed themselves to the project, the initial one-day
workshop covers an introduction to feminist concepts, an interdisciplinary discussion of feminist theory, and a presentation about curriculum integration. The final part of the workshop is devoted to review
of model course syllabi "before and after" revision.

Orientation Workshop Program
Women's Studies, University of Arizona
NEH Curriculum Integration Project

Project Director: Myra Dinnerstein
Assistant Director: Judy Lensink

9:00–9:30 A.M.	Introduction to Women's Studies Concepts—Sidonie Smith
9:30–10:30	Panel: Sex Role Asymmetry Psychological/Biological—Patricia MacCorquodale Religious/Mythic/Literary—Susan Aiken Economic/Historical—Karen Anderson
10:45–11:45	Discussion of Readings:

Rosaldo—   "Women, Culture, and
                     Society: A Theoretical
                     Overview"
Chodorow— "Family Structure and
                     Feminine Personality"
Ortner—   "Is Female to Male as
                     Nature Is to Culture?"
Pateman—   " 'The Disorder of
                     Women': Women, Love
                     and the Sense of Justice"

12:00–1:00 PM	Lunch
1:00–2:00	"What Do We Mean by Curriculum Integration?"—Janice Monk
2:30–3:00	"A Celebration of Women Artists"— Margaret Brand

The Rosaldo, Chodorow, and Ortner articles are from *Woman, Culture, and Society,* edited by Michelle Z. Rosaldo and Louise Lamphere (Stanford: Stanford University Press, 1974). The Pateman article is from *Ethics* 91 (October 1980): 20–34.

On some campuses, project leaders have chosen to design seminars using the research on classroom interaction. This topic enabled faculty to look at their own behaviors in the classroom and to begin to understand the nature and extent of sex bias in the educational system. A resource that is particularly effective is the paper "The Classroom Climate: A Chilly One for Women?" (#77). Prepared by the Project on the Status and Education of Women, it documents and describes the parameters of the issues and offers concrete recommendations for change. Discussion of bias in the classroom can lead to the consideration of problems with textbooks and ultimately to discussion of the methods by which we shape the content and methodology of teaching.

4

Sustaining the Project

Strategies must be devised *early* in the project planning stages to sustain it until the long-term goals are achieved. Project leaders should keep the long-term vision of the project in their own minds and before the eyes of the faculty. The project should not be too closely identified with one set of short-term goals to avoid a premature end before major curricular reform is achieved. It may be possible at the outset to negotiate released time for an administrator or faculty member to oversee the continuing curricular reform to incorporate the study of women throughout the curriculum as part of her or his normal, assigned duties.

WORKING WITH FACULTY

Faculty who participate in curriculum integration projects need a clear understanding of what is expected of them: the goals of participation, how much time will be spent in seminars or reading groups, whether a specific product is expected when participation in formal activities is officially over, and how their work will be evaluated. This information should all be conveyed at the outset of the project. It is easier to require some sort of written "product" if tangible rewards, such as stipends or merit points, are associated with participation, but even in cases where such remuneration is not given, some concrete result of participation can give faculty a sense of accomplishment.

Providing a forum for faculty to present the results to peers is one way to provide them with visibility and recognition. The University of Utah used the occasion afforded by the final project meeting of the Northern Rockies Program, held on their campus, to sponsor panels at which faculty participants could present the results of their work for an audience of peers from throughout the region. Other campuses held informal seminars for faculty to present their revised syllabi to one another.

Another strategy is to write a formal letter describing their contribution to the project or to their field, with a copy to their department head and/or dean. These letters of evaluation can play an important role in promotion and tenure decisions. It may also be possible to call the attention of outside consultants to the work of specific faculty so they can write letters of support if needed.

Well-timed provision of resources to faculty is another means of sustaining them in their work. Project leaders might schedule an informal meeting with individual participants once per term to discuss the progress they are making in their course revision and use this meeting as a means of suggesting further resources.

One issue that surfaces repeatedly in curriculum integration projects is that of *quality control*. Project directors of several of the major projects designed to produce materials for a national audience found that faculty work often duplicated earlier women's studies research and was not reflective of the most current feminist scholarship. Some faculty did not take the work seriously, or abandoned their curricular reform efforts after they realized, in Howe's words, "the extent of the revolution"[1] embodied in feminist scholarship. Hence, project leaders had to strike a balance between rewarding good faith efforts and sustaining faculty in their intellectual growth, and criticizing work or suggesting further revisions of material that is not intellectually sound or current. Myra Dinnerstein maintains that quality work will only be achieved if the project director is willing to abandon a collegial role and assume one of standard-setter for faculty participants.[2]

In some cases, project directors were faced with the necessity of terminating a faculty member who was not living up to the expectations of the project. This is particularly difficult in cases where some financial or merit reward must be withheld. For this reason it is important at the outset of the project to make a formal agreement, preferably in writing, as to the nature of the product that is expected, when it is due, and how it will be evaluated. Some projects found it useful to establish a formal contract or letter of agreement with faculty; in less formal situations, general informational handouts to all participants sufficed.

UTILIZING STRENGTHS OF EXISTING ORGANIZATIONS

Resources for sustaining the project and accomplishing its goals can be expanded through the strengths and resources of existing committees and organizations. Regional consortia can be of particular help in providing an umbrella organization to support local projects. The Great Lakes Colleges Association Women's Studies Program provides a good example. The establishment of the Program in 1976 provided the opportunity for consortial cooperation in women's studies development among the twelve small liberal arts schools belonging to the Association whose individual resources would not have allowed for the development of women's studies programs along the lines of those in larger universities. Each year the GLCA Women's Studies Program sponsors a women's studies conference, and the visibility afforded by GLCA sponsorship lends legitimacy to local campus efforts both to develop women's studies courses and to integrate women's studies into the curriculum.[3]

The Northern Rockies Program was set up to facilitate cooperative relationships among several existing organizations. Using the Northern Rockies Consortium for Higher Education and the Northwest Women's Studies Association as sponsoring agencies of the Program on Women in the Curriculum was an important strategy. Both of these organizations had existing communication networks and programs that could serve as resources for the new project. Both were already committed to curricular reform, although with different emphases. And both were anxious, because of shrinking resources, to cooperate with a new program that would assist them in carrying forth some of their own program objectives. Each organization had its own newsletter that carried articles on the project, so resources for a new newsletter were not necessary.

Every school belongs to some organization. If a regional organization is not receptive to project goals, state caucuses of professional organizations can be sought as cosponsors for a discipline-based effort. This external validation can be extremely important to establishing the credibility of the effort.

In the same way, on individual campuses, standing committees and existing programs can be used as administrative locations to launch a new program. The women's studies program or faculty development program are, of course, ideal places for such an effort to be housed. Sustaining a project on a campus with an active women's studies faculty is a much easier task than on a campus where there is no such program or network of faculty. In the latter case, the short-term project goals must inevitably be the creation of a base of operation for longer-term change.

USING CONSULTANTS EFFECTIVELY

Creating a regional program and awarding mini-grants in a competitive process to institutions was a strategy that provided external visibility and credibility for local efforts. Local project directors used this external resource both as a carrot and a stick. The site visits I made as Program Director served to assess and reaffirm the commitment of key administrators to the project and iron out problems in communication between the various actors in the program. Project participants, supporters and detractors, are often more willing to raise concerns to an outsider than to project leaders, and the outsider may see problems or sources of additional support that the project team has overlooked.

Outside consultants can be used in a similar manner in campus projects. Wherever possible, persons brought in to make a presentation to faculty should also meet with administrators, board members, and participants on an informal basis and provide an assessment of project strengths and weaknesses from their own perspective. The consultants should bring a message that supports what local project leaders are attempting to accomplish. It helps, therefore, to brief them ahead of time about the current political climate of the institution, sources of controversy in relation to project goals, and any institutional history that is necessary for their understanding of the project. Send consultants material about the project in advance and specify the nature and content of their presentations. Be sure they understand the institution, the composition of the student body, and that of the faculty. It is always best to have heard the person speak or to have consulted someone who has in order to predict her or his effectiveness on your campus.

Outside consultants can also give a boost to project efforts by bringing a fresh perspective to a local effort and placing it in a broader context of what is happening regionally or nationally. They can inspire conversations between people or groups that normally do not interact with one another but have common goals and could work together for mutual benefit. They can carry messages from the faculty to the administration and can help explain the importance of the local effort to key groups. The outside consultant usually serves as an additional source of moral support for the project team by pointing out that their problems are not unique and that things are, in fact, going better than they think.

REWARDS FOR PROJECT LEADERS

On particularly bad days, when a parent has written to the president of the college to complain about the feminist orientation of your star faculty member's class, and the keynote speaker for the seminar you have been planning for six months calls up three days in advance and cancels, and you've been up every night after midnight trying to keep up with student papers, and your department head tells you that the promotion committee feels you're not doing enough publishing in mainstream journals, you wonder why you bother.

Recognition and rewards from colleagues and superiors are not normally reasons that project directors cite for having assumed this position. In fact, many of the project leaders in the Northern Rockies Program stated flatly that they had assumed the directorship in spite of the fact that it appeared to be a professional risk. What had prompted their decisions varied greatly. Most had a strong feminist commitment to work for change in higher education and saw curriculum integration as one important item on the agenda to achieve this change. This commitment was often expressed in terms of improving the educational environment for women students by raising the awareness of their colleagues to bias in the curriculum and in advising. Many leaders hoped to develop a new advocacy or support group for women's studies both on campus and in the region, which would help to overcome the isolation they experienced. For these women, the project appeared, through the human and financial resources it offered, as a survival strategy. To women's studies programs experiencing financial difficulty, the $2,000 Program stipend enabled them to offer outreach activities and further some of their goals.

Some project directors felt that their administration was firmly committed to the project and that it would afford them the opportunity to work on a project of importance to the institution. In two cases, faculty had assumed the role of director for the expressed purpose of developing leadership and management skills for future administrative work in higher education.

It is particularly important for project leaders to receive tangible rewards for their effort. This usually comes during a particularly successful seminar or workshop or when faculty convey the excitement of their intellectual discoveries. Using a team approach to management helped project leaders to sustain one another during the more difficult times and to take turns dealing with troublesome problems. Visiting speakers and consultants are also important sources of support and are usually mindful of writing to senior officials to call attention to the quality and importance of the local project.

ANTICIPATING AND COPING WITH RESISTANCE
Resistance to the incorporation of the new scholarship on women into the curriculum will arise from both faculty and students and it is important to anticipate it and to plan ways to handle it.

Faculty Resistance
In their response to feminist scholarship, faculty can be divided into three categories: the unreachable, the sympathetic but unknowledgeable, and the already committed and knowledgeable. A person's age or sex does not necessarily predict group membership. The first group is composed of faculty with an unwavering belief in the traditional standards of excellence that have shaped the curriculum and the current body of knowledge as representative of the best "man" has thought, created, and accomplished. This body of knowledge, they believe, has been generated through objective modes of research and scholarship. Women's studies, on the other hand, born out of a social change movement, is subjective and ideological. Its claims on the curriculum, if any, are based in sociology not epistemology. Women's studies represents only "a special interest group." These are the Phase 1 thinkers (see page 26).

These faculty may also be respected scholars in their field and popular teachers. They have no reason to change. If faced with pressure from administrators or project leaders, they will raise issues of academic freedom, the place of ideology in the curriculum, and their right to determine what is to be taught in their classes. Most project directors felt it was not worth the effort to target this group specifically, although some of its members, because of their political influence on campus, had to be consulted about the project and their approval sought.

2.   Faculty who are sympathetic to project goals may still have areas of resistance to overcome both personally and professionally. As Peggy McIntosh has warned, the new scholarship on women may be hazardous to your ego: "It calls into question not only what we thought we knew, but also what we as professors thought we were...basically intelligent, fair-minded, knowledgeable, alert to politics in the curriculum, and unique in our intellectual and pedagogical styles."[4] Discovering the systematic biases inherent in the method and content of our scholarship and in our teaching behaviors shatters this sense of professorial self. Coming to terms with the message of feminism also calls into serious question personal relationships, both on the job and at home. Some faculty, when they come up against the radical nature and the scope of the transformation that is necessary, lose heart and abandon their efforts at change. They may have been at Phase 3 thinking, and, rather than pushing on to Phase 4, revert to Phase 2. Others, while willing to accept the feminist analysis of traditional knowledge, may not apply the critique beyond a purely abstract realm and thereby demonstrate a profound lack of connection with the material and its implications for their personal and professional lives.

Professional considerations can pose very real barriers to faculty who are sympathetic to project goals. Over half of the faculty who participated in the MSU WEEA Project reported in their final interviews that they perceived the Project as a professional risk, and had encountered reactions ranging from indifference to outright hostility from colleagues. Eight of the thirty-six faculty interviewed reported that they had joined the Project in spite of negative attitudes of deans or department heads. This pattern was replicated in several of the projects in the Northern Rockies Program. Project directors reported having difficulty recruiting even sympathetic faculty who were afraid of the visibility the project would provide (they were willing to be "underground" supporters of women's studies) and afraid of losing their credibility with their colleagues. Several project directors felt strongly that they should not seek to involve untenured faculty in such projects.

These fears have some basis in reality. They can be partially mitigated by having strong administrative support for the project, piggy-backing on a "legitimate" institutional program, and by the participation of a broad base of faculty. Another strategy is to involve an entire department, as did the program at Western Wyoming College, or all the faculty teaching similar courses, so that a colleague support system emerges. Engaging only one participant per department leads to isolation and professional liability. The Wheaton College program, in an effort to ensure that faculty participants had assessed the degree of support of their colleagues, asked, as part of the application process, how departmental colleagues could be brought into the effort.[5]

One of the greatest barriers to faculty who are sympathetic, but unknowledgeable, may be, ironically enough, the breadth and scope of the new body of scholarship on women itself. It is no longer possible to spend a few weeks "brushing up" on the material in order to revise a course. Becoming familiar with the new scholarship on women relevant to one's field is now more like obtaining a new doctorate.[6] Few faculty will make this commitment; and those who do will have to spend considerable time getting caught up. One of the faculty in the Wheaton program stated the problem clearly:

> But [the program] also made me realize how little I knew, how many books I had to read, how many books I had to re-read, and—most disturbing—how I had to reconsider the values that governed the canon and approaches to which I've been committed in my teaching and writing. We know that such radical re-evaluation should be ultimately enlivening, but not until we go through the very hard work and very real doubting.[7]

There is also a sub-group of sympathetic faculty who can be troublesome. These are the faculty who think they have *already changed* and who join the project to tell *others* that *they* must change. One project director described participants in her project this way:

> Faculty signed up to be experts; they did not sign up to undergo changes themselves. Their lives are heavily invested in not taking women seriously; usually nothing short of a conversion experience, or out-and-out, individualized, personal discrimination will make them change their attitudes; and then they become fighters, not feminists...Asking a "liberal" to examine his sexism is a crime second only to ignoring him while he does so.

Unexpected resistance may surface from women's studies faculty who worry, quite legitimately, about what happens to the feminist perspective when material is taught by faculty not thoroughly versed in the content and methodology of women's studies. Will students get

only a superficial treatment of the material and yet feel that they have
covered the subject? Will what is taught about women include and reflect differences of race, culture, class, and sexual identity? Will hierarchical structures be broken down in the classroom? Arguments that
women's studies as a field has itself not yet been sufficiently genera-
tive or inclusive of all women and that the energy of feminists should
be directed toward the end of creating a truly multicultural, multiclass
women's studies are also compelling.[8]

The question may become particularly divisive on campuses where
a curriculum integration project is launched in a top-down mode from
an administrative location other than an existing women's studies program and without consulting women's studies faculty. It should become clear to administrators from the outset that curriculum integration and women's studies are not either/or choices and that building
a strong, permanent women's studies faculty is the best base from
which to begin a curriculum integration effort.

Student Resistance

Student resistance to material on women should also be anticipated. Over half of the MSU faculty who revised their courses to incorporate new scholarship on women reported hostile, negative, or
defensive reactions on the part of at least some of their students.[9]
They perceived resistance to stem from several sources. According to
the faculty, students had already developed a good sense of what the
course was "supposed to" cover, and resented what they perceived
to be a deviation from the norm. The material also threatened their
world view by questioning the traditional assumptions of society and
culture. With the increasing emphasis toward professional preparation, students are less likely to respond positively to material that does
not appear to meet immediate needs and further challenges their sense
of self and their conception of what their lives will be like. In some
cases, students, including female students, felt that the "problem"
had been solved, and that the faculty member was overstating the
case. Directors of projects at women's colleges corroborate this reaction from young women who feel that opportunities will no longer be
denied to them on the basis of their sex. They find feminism threaten-
ing to the comfortable future they envisage for themselves.

Student discontent seemed greater when faculty declared their
reasons for incorporating content on women instead of simply teaching the material as they would any other legitimate course material.
Some announced that they were participating in a special women's
project, hence "trying out" new material. Students apparently felt like
guinea pigs and expressed their desire for the unadulterated, "real"
version of the course. As faculty became more familiar with the ma-

terial, integrated it more, and taught it without calling attention to it, student discontent lessened.

In some cases, student dissatisfaction with courses incorporating substantial content on women expressed itself ultimately on course evaluations. Some MSU faculty reported lower evaluations than normal in courses they had been teaching for a number of years. It is therefore very important to alert department heads and deans to the nature of the changes in these courses and seek their support for teaching that challenges students to question underlying assumptions about society and culture. By the same token, informing faculty who are teaching feminist material for the first time about possible student reactions and suggesting teaching techniques for diffusing hostility will help prepare them for possible student anger in the classroom.

EVALUATING THE PROJECT

Most earlier curriculum integration projects, funded by external agencies that required documentation of program results, included formal evaluation components. The SIROW report on *How to Integrate Women's Studies into the Curriculum* (#30) contains a brief section on the evaluation strategies of the seventeen projects represented at the 1981 Princeton Workshop on Integrating Women's Studies into the Curriculum. Participants reported using a variety of methods to measure changes in faculty and in their courses: (1) pre- and post-project interviews with participants; (2) monitoring of project activities by staff; (3) pre- and post-project attitude surveys of faculty participants; (4) post-project surveys of student attitude change in experimental versus control group courses; (5) pre- and post-project review of syllabi; (6) oral and/or written reports by participants; and (7) project review by outside consultants or evaluators. However, specific information about evaluation design and results is found primarily in individual project reports to funding agencies; very little published literature exists on the evaluation of curriculum integration projects.

It is not my intent in this brief section to provide an introduction to the concepts, practices, and procedures of program evaluation, but rather to describe common evaluation components and issues that surface in curriculum integration projects. Several good introductions to evaluation in women's studies and women's equity programs exist. For the beginner, Ruth Exstrom gives a brief and very useful overview of evaluation terms and concepts, presents a model evaluation plan, and discusses purposes and kinds of measurement in her article on "Evaluating Service Learning Programs in Women's Studies" in #100. Mary Ann Millsap et al., *Women's Studies Evaluation Handbook* (#74), is also a good resource.

Deciding What to Measure and How to Do It

The projects participating in the Northern Rockies Program on Women in the Curriculum were not required to have a formal evaluation component and did not have budgets that would permit contracting for external evaluation services. Most project directors did, however, use various methods to obtain information for purposes of gauging the success of project activities and designing future activities.

Project leaders were most interested in measuring program impact on faculty and on the curriculum. The latter was at least superficially easy to do through quantitative measures such as counting the numbers of courses revised and new courses developed, and by noting any new policies or requirements implemented to ensure that courses include the study of women.

Other quantitative measures used to judge project impact included the number of faculty who attended faculty development seminars and the number of activities related to project work initiated by faculty, such as papers at professional meetings. Projects also looked for spin-offs, such as grants written by faculty related to women's equity, or changes in hiring patterns in specific departments. Even if the project team could not formally claim reponsibility for some of these changes, they documented them and used them for future planning and in reports or project publicity.

Measuring changes in faculty participants was a much more problematic task. Many of the projects had as stated goals the raising of faculty awareness about the new scholarship on women or about the nature and extent of sex bias in higher education curricula and the altering of faculty research, teaching, and advising behaviors. Trying to measure these changes in a scientific manner, however, raised issues of practicality and intrusiveness. Most projects relied on sympathetic faculty volunteers. Project leaders did not wish to impose evaluation techniques, such as attitude surveys, observation of classes, or student questionnaires that would make faculty unwilling to participate. On the other hand, project leaders were interested in ensuring some form of quality control in the new courses and having some means of assisting faculty in course revision on an ongoing basis. Leaders who did use these kinds of measures explained the evaluation plan to the faculty and obtained their consent at the outset of the project to administer evaluation instruments.

The most common method used to measure project impact on faculty was to review the courses they developed under the project. In most projects, faculty participants were willing to submit their revised syllabi to project leaders, but the latter were often reluctant to be too critical, or did not have enough expertise in certain areas to judge if the material was accurate or reflective of the latest research in the discipline. Project leaders struggled with several issues: Whose standards should be applied in this process of evaluation? What does a "transformed" course look like? How much material on women should be expected in a given course? Who should or can judge courses in specific disciplines?

It is a good strategy, where feasible, to have a third party or group to review and critique faculty work. This can be done by an outside consultant or even by the project advisory board. A feminist scholar coming to campus for a speaking engagement related to the project may be asked to review syllabi for courses or to meet individually with faculty who are experiencing difficulty. The Montana State University WEEA Project designated funds for a peer review panel composed of scholars in women's studies and faculty at MSU to review the course revision proposals of the faculty participating in the project. The panel presented a seminar for the group to discuss, in general terms, the strengths and weaknesses in the proposals. Panel members then met individually with faculty in their disciplines to critique their courses, propose revisions, and suggest further reading. Another successful process was implemented at the University of Wyoming, where the General Education Committee now reviews courses being proposed for the new set of requirements for relevant material on women and minorities. The committee uses faculty from women's studies as consultants on specific course proposals yet bears the responsibility for rejecting courses that do not include women and minorities in a significant manner.

Project leaders relied heavily on participants' perceptions to judge project impact. In most cases, participants were asked to fill out evaluation questionnaires that measured their degree of satisfaction with project content, project organization, the choice of speakers, and their perception of the relevance or usefulness of the activity to their specific needs. Project leaders then used these questionnaires to plan future seminars and to select materials for distribution to faculty as a follow-up activity.

Some project directors used visits by outside consultants as a means of formative evaluation for the project. Consultants were asked to meet with personnel and participants in the project and to provide feedback on their perceptions of the project. Reports from external visitors can be used to communicate both problems and successes to staff, participants, and administrators.

In all cases, project directors relied, by necessity, on inexpensive means of evaluating the project. Technical assistance in evaluation design had been available at the initial training institute held at Montana State University and several campuses took advantage of this opportunity. Others used faculty consultants on their own campuses or their advisory boards to help with the evaluation design and analysis of results.

In general, those project directors who used some form of formal evaluation expressed more satisfaction with project results than those who did not. The project team had decided early in the planning stages what outcomes they anticipated and selected simple measures to determine if they were achieving them. By collecting and reviewing these data, they were able to judge the degree of knowledge and satisfaction of the faculty participants, to modify plans for further activities, and to provide administrators with concrete evidence of project impact.

Representative Short-Term Outcomes

Short-term impact of participating projects occurred in a number of areas:

Network Development—Several campuses reported increased communication between different women's groups on campus; or between project leaders, faculty, and administrators. New networks for sharing information and resources developed on the campus, between nearby institutions, and among the project leaders from the ten campuses in the four-state region.

Faculty Awareness—Most project leaders reported increased faculty awareness of both the nature and extent of bias in higher education and of resources in women's studies available for course revision. Many faculty participants had already begun to do research in women's studies and to present papers on related topics at professional meetings.

Resource Development—One important result directly related to project efforts on several campuses was the development of improved access to the new scholarship on women. These improvements included increased library holdings in women's studies; the creation of a computerized data base to access materials on women; and establishment of a clearinghouse for model courses and materials.

Curriculum—Most projects aimed at changes in specific courses or curricular review procedures were able, by the end of the first year of the project, to report either the development of new courses focusing on women, the revision of several standard courses, or the establishment of a process to review courses for content on women.

Policies and Procedures Affecting the Educational Climate for Women Students—Several project directors reported changes in policies and procedures, such as improved advising for women students; restructuring of affirmative action procedures in an attempt to make them more effective; and allocation of internal resources for specific women's equity projects. In two cases, project directors related specific hiring of female faculty to the influence of the project.

Visibility of Women's Studies—Project activity on some campuses had the effect of increasing the visibility and legitimacy of women's studies and providing better contact with faculty colleagues and administrators. Specific examples include the approval of a women's studies course to fulfill general education requirements at the University of Wyoming and the coordination of offerings into an option for a self-declared minor in women's studies at the University of Montana.

Student Awareness—Several projects had components designed specifically for students, and project leaders reported impact on student awareness of sex bias and knowledge of resources to combat it.

Professional Development—In their exit interviews, several project directors mentioned their personal growth as administrators as one measure of project impact. They had had concrete experience with managing a small budget, chairing committees, building coalitions, negotiating with administrators and faculty, evaluating their peers, and overseeing a complex change process.

NOTES

1. Howe, "Feminist Scholarship,"#8.
2. "Mainstreaming the Feminist Curriculum: Expectations, Problems, and Achievements." Talk delivered at the National Women's Studies Association meeting, Ohio State University, June 29, 1983.
3. Beth Reed, "Transforming the Academy: Twelve Schools Working Together," in #66.
4. McIntosh, "WARNING: The New Scholarship on Women May Be Hazardous to Your Health," #46, p. 29.
5. Spanier, in #66, p. 32.
6. Howe, "Feminist Scholarship," #8, p. 15.
7. Spanier, in #66, p. 33.
8. Johnnella Butler, "Minority Studies and Women's Studies: Do We Want to Kill a Dream?" in #22.
9. Schmitz and Williams, "Seeking Women's Equity through Curricular Reform," #60.

5

CONCLUSION

PROJECT IMPLEMENTATION: DO'S AND DON'TS

There is no one "best" strategy or mix of strategies that will ensure successful implementation of a curriculum integration project. In spite of careful planning, competent staff, and adequate resources, projects normally run into unforeseen difficulties and may fail to achieve some of their goals for reasons beyond the control of the project leaders. These include shifts in political power within the institution, low faculty morale, reorganizations of administrative units, loss of resources due to cutbacks or shortfalls, and well-mounted attacks from opposing groups that result in loss of administrative or faculty support. Other pitfalls and problems that lead to failure can be avoided if recognized early in the planning process. Projects also succeed due to a unique combination of predictable and unpredictable factors. Analysis of the outcomes of the ten projects participating in the Northern Rockies Program on Women in the Curriculum and similar projects yields, however, some insights into the "do's" and "don'ts" of project planning and implementation.

Don't:

• Set project goals that are too ambitious or too abstract.
• Set short-term goals with no longer term vision.
• Assume who is with you and who is against you (check it out!).
• Avoid essential intellectual and political issues.
• Try to accomplish too much too fast or with too few resources.
• Rely on token rather than real administrative support.

Do:

• Have strong, visible administrative support.
• Clearly define short and longer term goals and seek consensus among project leaders about project goals.
• Be informed by a long-term vision for change while undertaking concrete, achievable steps.
• Carefully assess the power structure and political climate of the institution.
• Carefully assess the level of interest and expertise of faculty.
• Allow adequate planning time.

- Confer with both interested groups of people *and* potential opponents of the project.
- Make alliances with appropriate groups on campus and in the community.
- Choose a project director with a solid background in women's studies, good leadership ability, tenacity, and patience.
- Form an advisory board to assist in needs assessment and project design and implementation.
- Develop an intellectually rigorous program of activities for the faculty.
- Provide clear criteria for faculty participation in the project.
- Formally evaluate project activities and make changes in implementation strategies based on sound evidence.
- Communicate regularly with all interested groups and take advantage of opportunities to publicize the project.
- Use existing external and internal resources effectively.
- Take advantage of existing procedures and processes to further project goals.
- Provide rewards for both staff and participants.

CONDITIONS FOR SUCCESS

The short term results of the ten Northern Rockies projects, especially those related to resource and network development, combined with the ability of project teams to capitalize on existing programs or institutional priorities, bode well for the accomplishment of longer term curricular change. They also help answer the question about how much change can occur with limited resources. On those campuses where, in addition to the $2,000 provided by the Program, there existed support from the administration, a core group of committed individuals, women's studies expertise and resources on campus, an impetus for reform and a specific opportunity for faculty development, and incentives to support faculty participation, a project could be launched to accomplish the following:

- to introduce the entire faculty or a core group to feminist scholarship and its implications for curricular change;
- to develop a core group of people to work for future change;
- to begin the process of course revision in specific departments or areas of the curriculum;
- to document curricular needs in women's studies;
- to acquire resources in women's studies; and
- to assess future resource needs to build up a project of more extensive faculty or program development.

The energies and commitment of the project leaders cannot be underestimated as the key element in the success of these projects. None of the project directors was salaried by the project budget; but most directors had positions in the institution that enabled them to take on the leadership of the project for a specific period of time. Using a team approach, hiring student research assistants on the project, and working within the framework of existing programs reduced the amount of time necessary for one individual to manage the process. Project activities had to be scaled, however, to the amount of time and energy available. The more extensive the project goals and activities, the more essential it is to build responsibilities for directing the project into the normal, assigned duties of the director and hence to negotiate salary or released time specifically for the project.

The projects also capitalized on the resources and support of the Northern Rockies Program. Without benefit of this external validation and support, project leaders would have had to invest more time initially in planning and seeking out sources of support. Fewer grants from federal and private sources are now available for women's studies. Future project leaders should assume therefore that most resources both for strengthening women's studies and for initiating curriculum integration projects will have to come from internal sources, such as deans' discretionary budgets and funds for faculty development or instructional improvement. A number of administrators have been exposed through national meetings to the rationales and results of projects to integrate women's studies into the curriculum and some are willing to reallocate internal resources. Project planners may also be able to identify state or regional agencies or foundations with priorities that projects of this nature can address. Other sources of potential funding include alumni foundations and student funds for program development.

Given these considerations, a checklist can be developed of essential conditions for initiating a project to integrate women's studies into the curriculum:

- a key group of committed individuals who will act as change agents
- administrative support for the project
- women's studies expertise and resources on campus
- resources to support faculty development activities
- an impetus for reform or specific opportunity for faculty development
- incentives for participating faculty
- a legitimate home base for the project within the institutional power structure, and
- salary or released time for a project director to oversee the effort for a specific period of time.

It should be kept in mind in project planning that with slim resources, limited energies, and multiple demands upon both, most institutions will probably not support both the development of a strong women's studies program where one does not already exist and a substantial curriculum integration project. Feminist educators working in institutions of higher education will thus have to make choices about strategy. Curriculum integration is obviously undesireable if it has the potential for weakening women's studies. A project should have the effect of establishing a women's studies presence on campuses where there currently is none, and where one does exist, of strengthening offerings, increasing the perceived legitimacy of the program, or extending its influence. In both programmatic strategies—women's studies programs and the faculty development projects aimed at general curricular change—institutions will have to commit resources to hiring and tenuring feminist faculty and to developing courses and curricula that are multicultural and inclusive in content and perspective.

PART TWO

Projects

6

The Northern Rockies Program on Women in the Curriculum

The project histories in this section were compiled and edited from the final reports and accompanying materials submitted by the directors of projects participating in the Northern Rockies Program on Women in the Curriculum at the conclusion of formal project activities in June 1983. The histories are arranged by type of project: projects to reform general education or core curricula; faculty development projects; projects to develop networks of faculty working on curricular reform; and projects to expand options for women in nontraditional fields of study.

For each project, the following information is included:

Institutional background, including location, size, and type of institution; enrollment and sex composition of the student body and faculty; history of women's programs; and current priorities for curricular reform.

Inception and definition of project, including needs addressed, impetus for reform, project goals, and composition of the project planning team.

Plan of action, including a description of project activities with emphasis on strategies to elicit faculty participation.

Short-term impact, a brief discussion of major areas of impact after initial project activities.

Future activities, a statement of future directions for change.

Project director, name, title, and address.

Sample materials from these projects may be found in Schmitz, *Sourcebook for Integrating the Study of Women into the Curriculum, #57.*

PROJECTS TO REFORM GENERAL EDUCATION AND CORE CURRICULA
Inclusion of the new scholarship on women in courses fulfilling general education requirements, in courses required of all students, and in core curricula for departmental majors confirms the centrality

of the study of women to undergraduate education. Three projects were designed toward this aim: **The University of Wyoming** project to encourage the inclusion of material on women and minorities in courses developed for the new College of Arts and Sciences general education program; **Western Wyoming College** to revise English and mathematics courses required of all students; and **Lewis-Clark State College** (Idaho) to revise courses fulfilling degree requirements in Management Technology.

The University of Wyoming
Women's Studies and General Education: Combining Forces

Institutional Background

The University of Wyoming is the only four-year institution of higher education in the state. It enrolls some 10,000 students; 8,000 of these are undergraduates, 45 percent female. Twenty percent of the 767 faculty are women. Seventy-five percent of the students come from Wyoming, including transfers from the state's seven community colleges.

In recent years, the University of Wyoming has had both the resources and the impetus to expand research and improve curriculum. In 1981 the faculty of the College of Arts and Sciences approved a proposal to revise the core curriculum. A General Education Committee was appointed to work with departments to implement innovative requirements in liberal education, to review proposed courses, and to coordinate community college courses with the university curriculum.

The University approved a Women's Studies Program in 1981 and a Women's Studies minor in 1982. From the outset, the mission of the Women's Studies Program, as stated in the charge from the Dean of Arts and Sciences, has been both to develop a curriculum of courses in women's studies and to design approaches to the incorporation into existing courses of women's issues and perspectives as embodied in women's studies research.

In 1981–82, the year prior to the project, the General Education Committee had sponsored a series of speakers on general education, and three of these, John Bonner of Princeton, Kenneth R.R. Gros-Louis of Indiana, and Carolyn Lougee of Stanford, had addressed the need to integrate women's studies into the curriculum. At the same time, the Women's Studies Committee had sponsored a series of speakers on research on women by women, including Kathryn Kish Sklar, Carol Nagy Jacklin, and Arlie Hochschild.

Inception and Definition of Project

The Wyoming project proposal to the Northern Rockies Program on Women in the Curriculum emerged as a joint proposal from the Women's Studies Committee and members of the General Education Committee to raise consciousness among a select group of faculty—the General Education Committee and the departmental representatives who advise on the development of courses for the general education program—about the new scholarship on women and its relevance to liberal education. (On reconsideration, the planning committee would now make portions of the program open to all interested persons.) The premise underlying the project was that the general education requirements being formulated should include a clear statement of support for the inclusion of women and minorities in the curriculum.

The objectives of the project planning team were to challenge assumptions about "objective" or gender-free disciplines; to encourage the General Education Committee to scrutinize courses proposed for general education with an eye to including women's perspectives; and to interest faculty in proposing courses for general education that significantly include women.

Certain factors favored a project of this nature at this time: a strong, supportive dean; sympathetic administrators of college-wide programs; an atmosphere within the College of Arts and Sciences conducive to major curricular review and innovation; close and cooperative relationships between members of the General Education Committee and the Women's Studies Committee; and the joint appointment of one member to both committees.

The project planning team included an administrative assistant to the Dean of Arts and Sciences; two faculty members from the Women's Studies Committee; and two members of the General Education Committee, one of whom is also on the Women's Studies Committee.

Plan of Action

The project's main activity was a two-day seminar to provide the General Education Committee and general education representatives from Arts and Sciences departments with research and perspectives on women. Since the major goal of the project was to raise consciousness among a select group of faculty—not to develop specific course proposals—the strategies used to recruit participants included: (1) a direct letter from the Dean to the General Education representatives of the twenty-seven Arts and Sciences departments requesting their presence or that of a substitute at the seminar; (2) two prominent speakers, one in the field of biology, one in literature; (3) an intellectually challenging series of events in which the focus was on general and conceptual issues; and (4) the scheduling of the seminar early in the fall semester before faculty became over-committed.

Science was chosen as the theme of the two-day seminar because, in the words of the project leaders, "Science is an area hardest to discern bias: people view it as objective."

The seminar began with a dinner for around sixty persons—faculty and spouses—on campus. Biologist Ruth Hubbard of Harvard University gave the keynote address focusing on social and sexual bias in scientific research. The seminar moved the next day to the University of Wyoming recreational camp, in a mountain setting. John Wideman, author in residence in the University of Wyoming English department, discussed redrawing the map of American Literature to include "minority" voices, imagining a "New World Literature." Following this, two concurrent workshops were held, one addressing women and minorities in the social science curriculum, and the other, women and minorities in Western civilization survey courses. Professor Hubbard concluded the day by returning to the issues of biased agendas in scientific research.

Short-Term Impact

Although a number of factors influence the General Education Committee's decision to return a proposed course for revisions, the project team reports that one factor that has been visible in several cases was the absence of material on women. Eleven courses including the study of women in a significant manner have been approved. Two of these are Women's Studies courses. Other Women's Studies courses are being prepared for submission.

Further measurable results are the naming of faculty with strong women's studies credentials as consultants on specific course proposals and the designing of a new Honors Program with a commitment to the inclusion of women in its readings and topics. Furthermore, the seminar itself gave the participants a common intellectual experience and resulted in the cooperation of people from different departments working together on course development. With respect to the General Education Committee, the project generated an atmosphere of support for issues, and the Committee now has a history of considering the inclusion of women and minorities as one criterion of academic legitimacy.

Future Activities

The project team has planned several ways to further their goals, such as keeping the issues visible with major speakers sponsored by both Women's Studies and General Education (in 1983–84 the theme of the Women's Studies speaker series was "The Woman Student"); continued informal discussions between members of the General Education and Women's Studies Committees; continued implementation of an Honors Program that is inclusive and has General Education credit; special attention to the fostering of women's talent in mathematics; and continued attention to the makeup of the General Education Committee.

Project Director
Janice Harris, Department of English, Hoyt Hall, University of Wyoming, Laramie, WY 82071.

Western Wyoming College
Desexing the Core: Curriculum Changes in Required Introductory Courses

Institutional Background
Western Wyoming College in Rock Springs is one of seven public two-year community colleges in the state system; it provides both liberal arts transfer programs and a comprehensive range of vocational courses. Western Wyoming College serves a predominantly older, commuting student population. The median age of the 1,264 students is twenty-eight; 70 percent of these commute. Approximately 60 percent of the students are women, over two-thirds of whom attend on a part-time basis. Fourteen of the forty faculty are women.

The college has implemented a number of services for these older, re-entry women students. There is a Women's Center that provides support groups, assertiveness training, counseling, and specialized study assistance. Courses on women offered through regular academic departments include Women in Literature, Women in History, Sex Role Stereotyping, and an Introduction to Women's Studies.

Inception and Definition of Project
The review of general education requirements at the University of Wyoming and the concomitant articulation of new requirements for in-state transfer students provided the impetus for curriculum changes in selected departments at WWC. For the first time, in 1983, students were required to take mathematics as well as English in order to transfer, and placement tests for transfers were instituted in both disciplines. These new requirements, along with the fact that beginning classes in both subjects are composed of a large number of older, returning women students, argued for a review and revision of these required, introductory courses.

The WWC project was conceived as a faculty development project with two principal goals. First, the project would make the mathematics and science faculty aware of the nature and extent of math anxiety among students, especially women students, and assist these faculty in introducing new methods and techniques into their classes. Second, the project would assist English Department faculty to integrate material on women into the required, introductory courses and thus help students, both male and female, to understand women's changing status in the world, as well as their past and present contributions. The two targeted English courses, required for the Associate of Arts degree, were Fundamentals of Composition and Basic Literary Types.

The project planning team consisted of the Dean of Academic Affairs; the Chairperson of the Humanities and Fine Arts Division, who has taught both required English courses and developed the Women in Literature course; the Director of the Women's Center; a faculty member in mathematics who supervises the Independent Study Laboratory; and a faculty member from English who serves on the departmental curriculum committee.

Plan of Action

The major strategy used to attract faculty was to provide special inservice activities for each of the two departments—mathematics and English—with outside consultants at the regular two-day faculty inservice training sessions held each fall. Faculty were sent materials about the topics for these special sessions ahead of time, along with a letter from the Dean urging their attendance. The prospect of discussing both substantive and practical teaching issues in their own disciplines with an outside "expert" was particularly appealing to faculty participants. At both the math and science and the English sessions, the large majority of faculty attended throughout the two days.

Sheila Tobias, author of *Overcoming Math Anxiety* (New York: W.W. Norton, 1978), conducted the session for the mathematics and science faculty. She provided an overview of the problem of math anxiety and its rootedness in elitist practices of teaching mathematics and science; conducted a demonstration with "math anxious" individuals; presented a series of techniques for helping students who are "math avoiders" and "math/science under-enrollers"; and discussed with faculty how they could implement specific changes in their teaching techniques. She also met with a group of campus and community women in an effort to assist with networking activities.

Jack Folsom of Montana State University's Department of English conducted a two-day workshop for English faculty on "Dealing in the Curriculum with Issues of Sexism." The first day's activities centered on assessing both instructors' and students' knowledge about sexism and attitudes toward conventional roles. The group designed writing assignments dealing with sexism and sex roles. During the second day, Professor Folsom treated issues of the literary canon and integrating literature by and about women into standard, required courses. The faculty spent the afternoon working on collaborative learning techniques for writing and literature classes and restructuring syllabi to incorporate materials and ideas from the seminar.

Short-Term Impact

The project team reports changes both in teaching techniques and attitudes among faculty as a result of the two seminars. The majority of the English faculty have incorporated new material on women in their courses and adopted collaborative learning techniques that help break down the authoritarian structure of the classroom. Faculty who have adopted these techniques report that their students are "learning to work with other students of different backgrounds, races, sex and ages in a collective effort to improve their writing." Moreover, WWC English faculty devoted each of their faculty meetings in 1983 to discussion of such topics as nonsexist teaching methods and strategies, choosing nonsexist textbooks, and using nonsexist language in the classroom.

The mathematics and science faculty appear more sensitive to the needs of "math anxious" individuals and have cooperated more readily in guiding them toward alternative learning situations.

Future Activities

The project team did not report on follow-up activities.

Project Director

Barbara Smith, Chairperson, Division of Arts and Humanities, Western Wyoming College, Rock Springs, WY 82901.

Lewis-Clark State College
Integrating Content on Gender into the Management Technology Core

Institutional Background

Lewis-Clark State College is the smallest four-year institution in the Idaho state system with an enrollment of about 2,000 students. The College is both an Area Vocational Technical School and a liberal arts college. The student population is 57 percent female; twenty of the fifty-one full-time faculty are women.

Since 1978, Lewis-Clark has had an experiential learning program through which working adults can earn up to fifty-six credits for prior life experience. Competencies and experiences are documented in a portfolio and the credits earned through this process are applied toward a degree in Management Technology. The remaining credits toward this degree can be taken at a number of locations throughout Northern Idaho. Students participating in this program have accounted for significant enrollment increases at Lewis-Clark.

The College has no women's studies program or women's center. Programs and services for women students are furnished primarily through community groups and through regional projects carried out in cooperation with the University of Idaho.

Inception and Definition of Project

Analysis of student participation in the Portfolio Degree Program in Management Technology showed that 51 percent of the students enrolled between 1978 and 1982 were women. Many of these students were already employed in supervisory positions, and the majority intended to pursue careers in management. Required courses in the Management Technology core, traditional in nature, included little or no information designed to meet the needs and experience of these students or acquaint them with the history of women in the workforce and issues for women in management.

A project planning team composed of the Academic Vice President, the Assistant to the Dean of Continuing Education, who supervises the Portfolio Program, and selected faculty prepared a proposal to integrate the study of women into the curriculum of the Management Technology core and submitted it to the Northern Rockies Program on Women in the Curriculum. The hiring of a new Department Head for the Business Division provided the opportunity for new direction in this division, and the project team hoped to direct activities within the Division toward faculty development in women's studies.

Plan of Action

The project had three components. The first activity was a faculty development seminar for the Business Division on integrating materials on women's issues into courses in management. Donna Stringer, Director of the Office for Women's Rights, City of Seattle, made a presentation to the faculty and provided materials and bibliographies for use in course revision. During her two-day consultancy on campus, she also met with administrators, division heads, selected faculty members, and community women. She presented information on subjects related to both the status of women on campus and course and program development.

The Northern Rockies program director was present for these activities, and assisted in providing follow-up materials to division heads interested in curriculum reform. The question of classroom interaction was of particular interest to this group and the paper "The Classroom Climate: A Chilly One for Women?" (#77) was distributed to all division heads, departments, and administrators.

The second component of the project was the acquisition and provision of women's studies materials to selected faculty undertaking course revision. The project purchased "The Tale of O," a slide-tape presentation prepared by Rosabeth Moss Kanter and associates. This resource was used in several classes in the Management Technology core as an introduction to sexism and racism in communication patterns. The project also purchased *Women's Studies Abstracts* as an addition to the library collection in women's studies.

The final project activity was a conference for students on "Coping Skills for Women in the Workplace." Donna Stringer returned to campus to deliver the opening address on "Issues for Women in Management." Other topics discussed at the conference included stress and working women, networking for women, and participatory management models. Forty off-campus adult women students attended.

Short-Term Impact
The student conference was successful in initiating a support network for women who tend to remain isolated in the workplace. Dealing with topics similar to those being integrated into courses helped students relate their life experiences with course material and provided further impetus for faculty to integrate material on women into their courses.

The Business Division currently has no female faculty members. At the outset of the project, faculty expressed a general lack of knowledge about the new scholarship on women and women's issues pertinent to the courses they were teaching. Although no major course revisions occurred during the first year of the project, participating faculty became more knowledgeable about the issues, more aware of the scholarship, and some have begun to integrate a few new materials, such as the slide-tape show, into their courses.

Future Activities
The second phase of activity related to integrating content on women into the curriculum will expand efforts to other departments outside of the Business Division. One of the required all-faculty workshops in 1983-84 will be devoted to this topic and faculty development funds will be sought to provide faculty with resources for course revision.

Project Director
Katherine G. Aiken, Assistant to the Dean, Continuing Education, Lewis-Clark State College, Lewiston, ID 83501.

FACULTY DEVELOPMENT PROJECTS
Faculty development is central to all projects to integrate women's studies into the curriculum. Included in this section, however, are those projects in the Northern Rockies Program with primary goals to increase the knowledge of the general faculty, or a core group, about the new scholarship on women, rather than to target a specific area of the curriculum. In these projects, faculty participated in semi-

nars on feminist scholarship and then revised courses they regularly taught.

In the **Central Wyoming College** project, two general inservice meetings on topics related to sex bias in curricula were held for the entire faculty; a core group of faculty was then selected as project participants based on a call for proposals for course revision. An all-faculty seminar covering various aspects of feminist scholarship and teaching was the core activity of the **Southern Utah State College** project; follow-up activities included providing resources and research assistance to faculty who received Title III grants for review and reform of courses in departmental curricula. **The University of Utah** Women's Studies Committee designed and implemented a mentoring model through which women's studies faculty worked with departmental colleagues on the revision of standard departmental offerings. Each of these projects devised specific strategies for faculty development in the light of unique institutional characteristics and current priorities for curricular reform.

Central Wyoming College
Integrating Women's Studies into the Central Wyoming Curriculum

Institutional Background
Central Wyoming College in Riverton is one of seven public two-year community colleges in the state system and serves an area of 30,000 square miles, including the Wind River Indian Reservation. Of the College's 522 students, 62 percent are women; 13 of the 44 faculty members are women. About 60 percent of CWC students attend part-time; of these, 73 percent are women.

In recent years, Central Wyoming College has undertaken specific program development activities aimed at instructional improvement. The College received a major grant from the National Telecommunication and Information Administration to construct a local telecommunications facility. The College has also been active in the Northern Rockies Consortium for Higher Education (NORCHE) and has committed internal funds for faculty development grants.

Central Wyoming College has no women's studies program; one women's studies course, Women in Literature, is offered on a regular basis through the English Department.

Inception and Definition of Project
The lack of programs and courses for women at CWC, combined with the increased enrollment of women students, particularly part-time and older women students, argued for a program to support curriculum and faculty development in women's studies. The project planners identified two goals: (1) to raise the knowledge of the faculty about sex bias in the curriculum and about women's studies research

and scholarship; and (2) to develop expertise in women's studies among a selected group of interested faculty who would revise standard courses or introduce new courses focusing on women into departmental curricula.

The project planning team included the Dean of Faculty and two faculty members in Political Science and Business. During 1981-82, these two faculty members began to restructure courses in their disciplines: Government of the United States and Wyoming, required for all students in degree programs, and Introduction to Business, taken by 40 percent of all majors in the Business and Industry Division. The Dean of Faculty resigned from the College in spring 1982 and was replaced on the team by a faculty member in English.

Plan of Action

A general workshop for all faculty on sex bias in the curriculum was held in September. The project team conducted the meeting in an informal fashion and presented information on bias in textbooks and how to counteract bias in the classroom. The two courses that had been revised the previous year were presented as examples of how to integrate material on women into standard courses. Participation in the workshop was voluntary, and most faculty attended and stayed throughout the day-long meeting.

The project team secured matching funds from the faculty development program to award merit points to faculty for project participation. The original plan was to call for a round of proposals for course development following the inservice seminar in September. However, a series of resignations and subsequent reorganization of duties among upper level administrators delayed implementation of the project.

A second faculty workshop was held in January 1983 on the topic of classroom interaction and differential treatment of female and male students. Shortly after this workshop, the call for proposals for course development was sent out. Five proposals were submitted and accepted: two from the Humanities; one from Counseling; one from Continuing Education; and one from Horsemanship. The selected faculty, along with the project team, formed an ongoing study group to read material in feminist theory and women's studies and assist one another in developing courses to integrate the study of women into the curriculum. They met six times during the first year of the project.

Short-Term Impact

During 1982–83, project leaders worked with three different academic deans and two different presidents. Implementing the project in the midst of multiple changes in administration was not an easy task, and the project team had to revise expectations of what could be accomplished in terms of curricular reform. Two immediate out-comes were apparent, however: (1) the sensitizing of the general faculty to issues affecting women students; and (2) the creation of a core group of faculty committed to educating themselves about the new scholarship on women in their disciplines and to integrating new material into their courses.

Another result was the emergence among the participating faculty of the desire to work toward more egalitarian institutional policies and procedures. This goal, and the development of a full range of courses on women in the College's curriculum, constitute the project team's long-term vision.

Future Activities

The major emphasis for future project activities will be in sustain-ing faculty interest in women's studies and supporting the creation of courses focusing on women. The project team will work to secure faculty development funds from internal as well as from external sources to support further development of women's studies at CWC.

Project Director

Patricia Corner, Division of Business, Industry, and Human Serv-ices, Central Wyoming College, Riverton, WY 82501.

Southern Utah State College
Curriculum Equity Project

Institutional Background

Southern Utah State College is an open-admissions institution that serves a rural population: half of the College's 2,400 students are from five southwestern Utah counties. The student body is currently 48 per-cent female. Twenty-one percent of the College's 121 faculty are women. The College is located in the small, predominantly Mormon community of Cedar City.

The College has no women's studies program. A Women's Re-source Committee, founded in 1972, regularly sponsors workshops, speakers, and films related to women's issues. Since 1975 the Com-mittee has sponsored a two-credit academic Women's Issues course each term. Topics have included: Women in Law; Women in the Arts; Women in Literature; Women in Utah History; and Many Sisters: A Cross-Cultural Perspective.

In 1981, the College received a three-year federal grant under Ti-tle III of the Higher Education Act of 1969 to review and reform the college curriculum. Under this program, thirty-two faculty received one-quarter academic leaves to review and revise three courses in their departments. Other factors contributing to an atmosphere conducive to change included new administrative leadership and a 14 percent growth in enrollment between 1981 and 1983. The new administration is charged with strengthening the liberal arts program and doubling the current college enrollment. The college has actively sought opportunities for interinstitutional exchange through membership in the Northern Rockies Consortium for Higher Education (NORCHE).

Inception and Definition of Project

These changes in administration and mission, along with the opportunity for faculty development provided through the Title III grants program, provided the impetus for initiating a program on women in the curriculum. The campus representative from NORCHE, in consultation with the Assistant Vice President for Academic Affairs and women active in local and regional women's groups, chose a three-member planning team and a broadly based advisory committee, composed primarily of tenured faculty and department heads, to assist the project team. The original team was composed of the president of the Faculty Senate; the Library Director, who is also on the Women's Resource Committee; and the administrator of the Special Services Program. The latter two team members report directly to the Assistant Vice President, who supervises the Title III Grant Program. The NORCHE representative later replaced the Special Services Director on the project team.

The primary goals of the project were (1) to raise the awareness of the general faculty, and more specifically those receiving academic leaves for course revision, to the need for the incorporation of the study of women and minorities into the curriculum, and (2) to provide resources and technical assistance to faculty who indicated an interest in revising courses to include women and minorities. The main vehicle for accomplishing these goals was a two-day faculty workshop in September 1982.

Plan of Action

In February 1982, to gauge the level of awareness of and support for nontraditional roles for women, the project team administered the Short Form of the Spence and Helmreich Attitude Toward Women Scale (see Section 1, note 4) to the entire SUSC faculty. The administration of this attitude survey, along with the selection and convening of the project advisory board, proved to be controversial, provided immediate visibility for the project on campus, and served as a major first step in heightening the awareness of faculty to issues of educational equity. To air concerns raised by these activities, an issue of the faculty newsletter, *Of Common Concern*, was devoted to the topic of gender-balancing the curriculum.

The planning and implementation of the fall faculty workshop, "Academic Excellence through Curriculum Development," was delegated by the Faculty Development Task Force to the project team. Additional funding for the workshop was secured from the Multi-Cultural Center, the Women's Resource Committee, the Utah Association of Academic Professionals, and NORCHE. This was the first full-faculty workshop in five years, and the Academic Vice President required that all faculty and deans attend. An invitation to participate was also extended to the faculty of nearby Dixie College.

Six outside speakers were invited to address topics related to general education reform for integrating women's studies into the liberal arts. Because faculty attendance at the workshop was required, the program was designed to provide for a variety of interests and a certain degree of choice. All faculty heard the three keynote speakers, two of whom addressed women's issues in the curriculum. The presentation that sparked the most debate among faculty was that of Lynda Sexson, a faculty member in Religious Studies at Montana State University, who argued the necessity of iconoclasm, breaking the images of the patriarchy, and not merely adding information on women to a biased body of knowledge.

Participants selected from concurrent sessions in the afternoon and on the second day. Each of these sessions was chaired by a member of the Faculty Development Task Force. Faculty were also able to schedule sessions with the outside consultants to get help in revising standard courses or developing new offerings.

At the beginning of the workshop, each faculty member received a discipline-specific packet of materials prepared by the project staff for integrating the study of women into courses in their disciplines. The final workshop session was devoted to reviewing practical information about the goals and anticipated outcomes of the faculty leave program.

In addition to this workshop, two formal meetings were held during the 1982–83 academic year for faculty on Title III grants to acquaint them with additional women's studies materials.

Short-Term Impact

Project activities were successful in raising the awareness of the general faculty to both the need and resources for incorporating the study of women into the curriculum. The workshop provided a forum for the discussion of issues and a mechanism by which those faculty interested in reform could identify colleagues with whom to work and resources to assist them in research and curriculum development. Ninety-three percent of the faculty who completed evaluations of the workshop expressed their overall satisfaction with the event.

Other changes related to the project's presence on campus have occurred. The President reaffirmed the institution's commitment to affirmative action and reactivated and expanded the role of the Affirmative Action Committee. Several courses have been substantially revised to incorporate the study of women, and a member of the Business Department developed and taught a Women in Management course for the Women's Resource Committee. In the future, this course will be taught as a regular offering of the Business Department.

Future Activities

The project team and advisory board will continue to work with faculty who receive Title III grants for course review and reform. Formal seminars on integrating the study of women and minorities into the curriculum are planned, and a collection of women's studies materials in the library is being augmented to assist faculty in research and curriculum development.

Project Director

Diana T. Graff, Director of the Library, Southern Utah State College, Cedar City, UT 84720.

The University of Utah
Women's Studies Mentoring Project

Institutional Background

The University of Utah, located in Salt Lake City, is by far the largest university in the Northern Rockies region, enrolling 20,600 undergraduate and 3,700 graduate students. Forty percent of the undergraduate student population is female; 20 percent of the 1,381 faculty are women.

The Women's Studies Program at the University was formalized in 1977 through a grant from the National Endowment for the Humanities. In 1979, the program was adopted by the College of Social and Behavioral Science and began offering both a minor and a major concentration. The current Women's Studies curriculum is organized as a special interdisciplinary program with a core of nineteen courses; about fifty courses are cross-listed each year between other departments and Women's Studies.

The University also houses a Women's Resource Center, which sponsors a number of courses and conferences each year, and the regional office of Higher Educational Resource Services (HERS/West), which sponsors training seminars and offers technical assistance to women in higher education administration.

Inception and Definition of Project

The call for proposals from the Northern Rockies Program on

Women in the Curriculum coincided with expansion of the goals of the Women's Studies Program. While affirming its major functions to design and sustain courses that focus on women and to coordinate a curriculum for a major and a minor in Women's Studies, the Women's Studies Committee recognized the need to integrate the study of women and gender into a wide range of courses and to create a network of faculty involved in feminist research.

The original project proposal called for activities to integrate the study of women and gender into the University's Liberal Education Program. When this did not prove feasible, the project coordinating committee adopted a proposal by which committee members would mentor willing colleagues in their respective disciplines. The aims of the mentoring project were: 1) to inform selected colleagues about issues of gender and the curriculum, 2) to guide these colleagues as they reconceptualized their courses to include women, 3) to direct colleagues to appropriate resources, and 4) to establish a bond that would support the actual implementation of the redesigned courses. The mentoring strategy was adopted to create a core group of faculty who could serve as conduits for integrating women's studies into the general curriculum.

The project was directed by the Chairperson of Women's Studies, and the Women's Studies Committee served as the project advisory board.

Plan of Action

During 1982–83, four Women's Studies faculty members in the departments of anthropology, English, political science, and sociology volunteered to work with five colleagues to revise departmental courses. The Women's Studies mentors approached colleagues whom they considered predisposed to the study of gender. Both the Women's Studies faculty member and the mentored colleague received small stipends and money for curriculum development.

The project faculty selected courses for revision either because of subject matter or because of the large numbers of students enrolled. These courses included Political Science 110 (American National Government), a department and university requirement offered twenty times per year and serving 1,500-2,000 students; Liberal Education 319 (Development in the Third World: Latin America), a course that fulfills requirements of the Liberal Education Program; English 271 (Critical Introduction to Literature), required of all English majors and a prerequisite to more advanced courses; and Sociology 331 (Social Change), taught twice per year at the undergraduate level and recommended for a specialization in social organization.

A meeting of the Northern Rockies Program on Women in the Curriculum held in Salt Lake City in May 1983 provided the occasion for the mentoring project teams to report on the results of their collaboration. A panel composed of the four departmental teams was scheduled and opened to the University of Utah faculty. Approximately forty faculty members attended. The mentored faculty and the Women's Studies mentors described their experiences in reevaluating course content, restructuring courses, and collaborating on the project.

Short-Term Impact

The project had the effect of broadening the base of support for Women's Studies and developing a new network of faculty doing research on women. In addition, the study of women and gender is now incorporated to some extent into two required courses at the undergraduate level: Liberal Education 319 (Development in the Third World: Latin America); and English 271 (Critical Introduction to Literature). Political Science 110 (American National Government) was revised to include a case study approach and to use women as examples when illuminating a concept, a principle, or a method of study. All three courses were taught for the first time in 1983–84.

A model for faculty mentoring was tested and refined to include criteria for the selection of faculty to be mentored, procedures for course revision and selection of materials, and guidelines for collaboration and team teaching.

Increased understanding among faculty as to the importance of teaching women's issues and perspectives may also have been a factor in the recent approval of two courses focusing on women for the Liberal Education Program.

Future Activities

The Women's Studies Committee, enlarged from eight to thirty-five faculty members, has submitted a proposal to an internal curriculum and research grant program to develop and implement study courses on integration for faculty in English and political science. In addition, an allotment for faculty development is being proposed for the Women's Studies budget to institutionalize the mentoring system.

Project Director

Margo Sorgman, Chairperson, Women's Studies Program, Room 205, Orson Spencer Hall, University of Utah, Salt Lake City, UT 84112.

NETWORKING OR CONSORTIAL PROJECTS

Two of the institutions participating in the Northern Rockies Program provide excellent examples of what Schuster and Van Dyne call the "bottom-up," coordination, or consortial curriculum integration model (see page 28). These projects originate with faculty and seek to connect and maximize internal resources and to do faculty outreach. They are networking projects that identify available human, material, and financial resources and unite previously dispersed feminist scholars and activists, and others new to women's studies, in specific change efforts. The joint **University of Idaho/Washington State University** project provides a model for faculty-initiated, interinstitutional exchange and development of resources in women's studies. The **University of Montana** model emphasizes both networking among women on campus and in the community and networking among faculty with similar research interests.

Both projects included male and female participants, staff, and faculty, and members of the larger feminist community. Both used a combination of informal networking and formal committee structures to accomplish change. These projects worked well in institutions with a critical mass of feminist faculty and shrinking institutional resources disallowing new efforts to initiate or expand women's studies programs.

University of Idaho/Washington State University
Women in the Curriculum: An Interinstitutional Program for Curricular Reform and Faculty Development

Institutional Background
Two major land grant institutions with a combined student population of over 20,000 collaborated on this project. The University of Idaho, in Moscow, has a student body of about 7,000 students, 37 percent female; 13 percent of the 370 faculty are women. Washington State, eight miles away in Pullman, has 13,700 students; 45 percent are women; 15 percent of the 783 faculty are women.

Severe cuts in higher education budgets in both states in the past several years have resulted in program cutbacks and curtailments at both institutions. The development of new programs within the next several years is highly unlikely.

Washington State University has a Women's Studies Program that offers an eighteen-credit minor and sponsors twenty courses cross-listed in seven departments. There is also an Office for Women's Programs and an active Association of Women Students. No formal women's studies program currently exists at the University of Idaho, although there are a number of feminist faculty members and several women's studies courses offered in academic departments.

Collaboration between women's programs at UI and WSU began in 1979, when the two universities planned and sponsored the annual Northwest Women's Studies Association (NWWSA) Meeting in Moscow. The NWWSA was codirected between 1980–82 by Sue Armitage, WSU Women's Studies Director, and Corky Bush, Assistant Dean of Student Advisory Services at UI. They also collaborated, along with Lewis-Clark State College, on an outreach program for rural women, funded by the Fund for the Improvement of Postsecondary Education, and a network to assist victims of domestic violence.

Inception and Definition of Project

At WSU, in spite of the existence of a strong Women's Studies Program, there has been no effort to include women's studies scholarship in traditional courses. At UI, faculty have consistently resisted concerted attempts both to establish a women's studies course list or to set up a program to integrate material on women into the curriculum. There was hence a need at both institutions to create greater recognition among faculty of the potential impact of women's studies and to develop a larger advocacy base of feminist faculty from which future change efforts could be launched.

The Women in the Curriculum Project was designed to meet four specific needs related to human and material resource development: (1) to develop support networks for faculty doing women's studies research or teaching, (2) to stimulate curricular review and reform, (3) to encourage individual and collaborative efforts in research related to women and gender, and (4) to develop resources for improving the quality of life for women students, faculty, and staff.

The project planning team consisted of the Women's Studies Director and the Dean of Social Sciences and Humanities at WSU; and, at UI, the Director of the New Dimensions Project for Rural Women, the Assistant Dean of Student Advisory Services, the Director of the Women's Center, and the Associate Dean of the College of Letters and Science.

Plan of Action

The main objective of the project was to encourage faculty to include the thought and experience of women in the standard curriculum by providing a program of faculty-initiated faculty development. Interinstitutional, interdisciplinary task forces were formed to address issues related to women in specific discipline groups: humanities, social sciences, medical studies, science and technology, creative and performing arts, professional schools, and advising.

Participation in these task forces was voluntary and was solicited through memos and personal invitation. Faculty were given no incentives other than the opportunity to learn about women's studies resources in their disciplines and to work on important issues in curricular reform. Project leaders coordinated the meetings of the task forces and assisted them in designing and implementing faculty development activities. A graduate assistant in the WSU Women's Studies Program developed a computerized data base of bibliographic materials in women's studies for use by faculty.

During 1982–83, task forces planned a number of faculty development activities. The Science and Technology Task Force published a summary of "The Classroom Climate: A Chilly One for Women?" (# 77) in the University of Idaho faculty newsletter and in the student newspaper and held a faculty workshop on classroom interaction. The Humanities Task Force secured funding from the Association for the Humanities in Idaho for a major conference on "Vision and Revision: Gender in the Humanities" held in Moscow in October 1983. This conference served as the lead-off for a speakers series to help UI faculty incorporate the study of women in their courses.

The Social Sciences Task Force sponsored a series of talks on both campuses by sociologist Barrie Thorne, and coordinated a workshop at the Idaho Sociological Association meeting on integrating women into the curriculum. The Advising Task Force developed an instrument to help advisees prepare for advising sessions, wrote and published a "Tips for Advisors" sheet to acquaint faculty with issues of bias in advising, and revised several college manuals to incorporate these new materials. These and other activities were supported by a monthly newsletter published on the UI campus and by the computerized Women's Studies Reference List developed at WSU.

Short-Term Impact

Immediate impact of the joint UI/WSU project is seen in a number of specific outcomes: several grant proposals, one funded by the Association for the Humanities in Idaho; the Women's Studies Reference List; the new advising resources for students and advising; and a new communication link, the UI newsletter.

As a result of these resources and the faculty development seminars, there has been a small but perceptible change in how women's studies research and activities are viewed on both campuses, such as greater faculty attendance at seminars and colloquia and more collaboration among faculty from different departments in research activities and grant application preparation. In addition, Women's Studies faculty and Women's Center staff have had, through the visibility afforded by the project, greater access to upper level university administrators than in the past.

The long range impact of the project on campus life may take several directions, including continued interest in women's studies colloquia and seminars, and an increase in the number of collaborative research and outreach projects. Although most of the original task forces have disbanded, the informal networks of faculty and staff will continue as viable sources of information, support, and specific, concerted actions.

Future Activities

The project directors will continue to publish the monthly newsletter as a vehicle to share information and resources. Washington

State University will hire a one-quarter-time graduate assistant to develop women's studies colloquia; a work-study student will periodically update the Women's Studies Reference List. In addition, the project will continue to sponsor a monthly speakers series bringing women's studies scholars to the two universities and will make resources and information available to faculty through other workshops, presentations, and informal contacts.

Project Directors
Corky Bush, Assistant Dean for Student Advisory Services, Women's Center, University of Idaho, Moscow, ID 83843; Susan H. Armitage, Director, Women's Studies Program, Washington State University, Pullman, WA 99164.

Project Coordinator
Mary Emery, Coordinator, New Dimensions Project, University of Idaho, Moscow, ID 83843.

The University of Montana
Women in the Curriculum Project

Institutional Background
The University of Montana in Missoula is a state-supported, four-year liberal arts institution with professional schools in Fine Arts, Law, Education, Forestry, Business, and Pharmacy, and several graduate programs. The current student population of 9,100 is 47 percent female; of the 477 full time faculty, 17 percent are women.

During the 1974–75 academic year, several women faculty and students developed a proposal to establish a women's studies concentration within the Liberal Arts degree program. The proposal was supported by the faculty senate, but was not funded and thus was never implemented. However, some of the women-centered courses proposed at that time are now offered: there are currently thirteen courses with a focus on women and fifteen additional courses that have been significantly modified to include women's issues. In addition, the Women's Resource Center independently developed a series of introductory and topical courses in women's studies taught by adjunct faculty.

Inception and Definition of Project
The 1981 call for proposals from the Northern Rockies Program on Women in the Curriculum provided the impetus for a core group of interested faculty and administrators to explore ways of increasing the impact of women's studies on the general curriculum and improving the status of women on campus. The two major needs identified by the planning committee were: (1) to coordinate and render more visible existing resources, including women faculty, women's organiza-

tions, women-related and women-focused courses, and library holdings; and (2) to integrate the study of women and gender into existing courses.

The project committee planned a group of activities to accomplish these goals: a survey of liberal arts departments to assess the degree to which faculty included material on women in their courses (accomplished in May 1982); a series of faculty development workshops on the new scholarship on women; a brochure describing women-focused courses; and the development and coordination of resources in women's studies.

The planning committee consisted of the Associate Dean of Arts and Sciences (Project Director), and faculty members from English, Social Work, Science Education, Business, and Library Sciences.

Plan of Action

As an official beginning for the project, an informal get-together was held at the Project Director's home for all interested women faculty and administrators. At this gathering, small committees were formed to oversee specific aspects of the project.

Two faculty workshops were held in the fall, one centered on the topic of women in science and one on bias in academic advising. At the former, Jan Raat of the Eindhoven Technical University of the Netherlands provided an international perspective on the topic of women in science; in the latter, faculty reviewed materials on avoiding bias in advising and discussed ways of expanding the aspirations of women students.

In October, the Project Committee co-sponsored the Northwest Women's Studies Association Regional Conference held on the University of Montana campus, and conducted panels on integrating women's studies into the humanities, social sciences, and sciences. Another major faculty development meeting was held the following April, attended by forty faculty members and administrators. The agenda included discussion of past and planned research on women at the University; presentation of an analysis of the status of women on campus; and a review of courses, textbooks, curriculum, and community resources in women's studies.

In addition to these core project activities for selected groups of faculty, the Project Committee also: (1) sponsored a Women's History Week exhibit in March; (2) co-sponsored a variety of presentations and films; (3) distributed a library resource on feminist periodicals to a targeted group of faculty; (4) supported two summer research projects for course revision; (5) and conducted a second survey of courses related to women. The Project Committee secured a special library allocation of $4,400 for purchase of books and other library materials to improve the women's studies collection and used this resource to enable project faculty to order new books in women's studies in their disciplines.

Throughout the academic year, members of the Project Committee worked to establish a process for diploma recognition for a program of study in women's studies through an upper division degree in Liberal Arts. In conjunction with the Women's Resource Center and an ad hoc Women's Studies Committee, the Project Committee submitted a request to the University Planning Council for a part-time position to coordinate women's studies offerings and teach an introductory women's studies course through the Humanities Division.

Short-Term Impact

The short-term impact of the project was seen in four areas: the development and revision of courses; planning for the establishment of a degree emphasis on women within Liberal Arts; the development and coordination of women's studies resources on campus and in the community; and networking of women faculty, staff, and administrators.

Course revisions to incorporate the study of women and gender occurred in several areas of the curriculum, including a three-quarter Introduction to Humanities sequence, the science education course for majors in secondary education, and selected courses in foreign languages, anthropology, social work, and sociology.

Faculty development workshops and seminars resulted in the formation of several permanent committees or groups, including a standing Women's Studies Committee established in cooperation with the Women's Resource Center; a library resources committee; and an informal group of women administrators who meet monthly at a no-host dinner to exchange information and ideas.

Within the Liberal Arts option, it is now possible on an individualized basis to fulfill upper division degree requirements with courses that focus on women and gender.

Faculty in various disciplines have also encouraged senior Honors Scholars to do research on women. Four honors projects focusing on women were funded in 1983. (Each Senior Scholar received a stipend of $1,200 and $250 for books and travel.)

Future Activities

A brochure on women's studies courses and resources at the University of Montana was distributed to all faculty, appropriate administrators and staff, and students during the fall 1983 registration period. The brochure will be updated with inserts annually.

The Women's Studies Committee will continue to coordinate activities to expand the impact of women's studies on the traditional curriculum. Committee goals include continued planning for a women's studies program; articulating a strong, cooperative relationship with the Women's Resource Center; encouraging faculty and student research on women and gender; supporting faculty development activities; and working to improve the status of women on campus.

Project Director
Maureen Cheney-Curnow, Department of Foreign Languages and Literatures, University of Montana, Missoula, MT 59812.

PROJECTS TO EXPAND OPTIONS
FOR WOMEN STUDENTS
An equitable and natural balance of women and men as students, faculty, and staff is as important to transformed educational institutions as a "balanced" curriculum. Eliminating artificial sex segregation in choice of field of study is critical to the attainment of this goal. Two projects funded by the Northern Rockies Program were aimed at expanding educational options for women students in nontraditional fields through combined programs of faculty and student development. The **Montana Tech** project targeted faculty and students in the engineering disciplines; **Weber State** was concerned with those in science and science education.

Montana College of Mineral Science and Technology
Project on Women in the Engineering Curriculum

Institutional Background
Montana College of Mineral Science and Technology (Montana Tech) in Butte, established in 1893 as the Montana School of Mines, offers degree programs designed to prepare students for professional service in the principal fields of raw material production. The College is growing rapidly and currently has over 2,300 students, representing an enrollment increase of 68 percent over the past four academic years.

At Montana Tech, the female student enrollment has been growing in recent years and currently constitutes 817 full-time and part-time students, an increase of 10 percent between 1982 and 1983. However, women students still comprise only 35 percent of the total student body and only 15 percent of the students enrolled in engineering curricula. Women make up 11 percent of the 106 full-time faculty.

There are currently no courses on women at Montana Tech.

Inception and Definition of Project
Recognizing the need to increase the representation of women students in the engineering disciplines, the College incorporated specific activities in its five-year plan of action adopted in September of 1980,

specifying a goal of 21.5 percent women students in engineering programs by 1985. Although considerable progress has been made in increasing the total number of female students at Montana Tech, the increase in percentage of female students in engineering has fallen behind scheduled projections.

In response to the 1981 Northern Rockies Program on Women in the Curriculum call for proposals, Montana Tech developed a Project on Women in the Engineering Curriculum to (1) increase the enrollment of women students in the engineering disciplines; (2) improve and equalize advising and career counseling services for women engineering students; and (3) increase the awareness of the Engineering Division's faculty to barriers to women students within existing curricula.

The project team consisted of the Academic Vice President, the Department Head of Engineering Science, a faculty member in Environmental Engineering (Project Director), and the Director of Cooperative Education and Intern Work Experiences.

Plan of Action

The project began with the premise that many women do not choose the engineering disciplines because of preconceptions fostered at the high school level or because of being intimidated by basic engineering terminology and principles typically presented through traditionally male-oriented examples. Two core project activities were planned: (1) the development and implementation of a freshman course, Engineering Careers, to present women with an introduction to technological concepts applicable in engineering; and (2) the presentation of a lecture series and seminars by women engineers to bring role models from the professional world to Montana Tech's students and faculty.

The Engineering Careers course was a new course developed in summer 1982 and offered in the following fall semester. It was designed to introduce students to the subject areas and career choices in engineering and to illustrate introductory concepts in physics, computer science, and mathematics used in engineering disciplines. In addition, a laboratory component introduced students to basic physical and mechanical principles in a hands-on manner. The course was coordinated by the Project Director and team-taught by faculty from each of the engineering departments. Through the participation of these departments, the lab sessions were conducted at a very low cost.

The Lecture Series with women engineers was offered once a month throughout the year beginning in November. Four of the five presentations were primarily non-technical, based on the engineer's experiences as a woman in an engineering discipline. Each lecture was advertised on campus through posters, memos to faculty/staff, the student and faculty newsletters, and letters to women engineering students. A women's service club on campus, the Spurs, assisted with the publicity, especially through word-of-mouth contacts with friends and classmates. Luncheons were held for most of the speakers to allow for an informal meeting with women students, faculty, and staff.

With the February speaker, the project committee used an additional strategy to recruit women into engineering. An engineering graduate from Montana Tech, who was also teaching and involved with research on campus, volunteered to go to the Butte junior high and high schools to meet with the girls in the science classes and encourage them to consider careers using math and science. In the spring, a conference on "Expanding Your Horizons in Math and Science" was held on the Montana Tech campus, co-sponsored by the project and the Sex Equality in Education (SEE) Institute of Rocky Mountain College in Billings. This conference brought women from the area to Tech to describe their math- and science-related careers to seventh- through twelfth-grade girls.

Short-Term Impact

The thirteen students in the Engineering Careers course were given pre- and post-class surveys to assess their degree of satisfaction with the course and its impact on their career choice. Student comments from the post-class survey showed that the course had not encouraged students to change their majors. The lab did provide a mechanism to introduce basic engineering concepts in a non-threatening manner and was judged valuable as an elective for engineering freshmen. It will become a regular part of the Engineering Science curriculum. Future recruitment of women students into engineering, however, will be concentrated at the junior high school level.

The course did have a noticeable impact on the faculty who participated. They became more conscious of barriers to women in courses where they are in the minority and learned techniques for encouraging and supporting equal participation of all students in classroom activities.

The project also made more visible to the college administration issues affecting the status of women on campus. More women have been appointed to faculty governance committees. The Academic Vice President purchased and distributed copies of "The Classroom Climate: A Chilly One for Women?" (#77) to all instructional staff and student services personnel.

Future Activities

The Project on Women in the Engineering Curriculum expanded its focus during 1983 and is now called the "Access for Women to Non-Traditional Careers" (Access) Project. The Access Project team, made up of women faculty and staff, has identified four major areas of activity for 1983-84: (1) outreach activities for girls and young women in the local community and their parents; (2) increased recruitment activities directed toward women in conjunction with the Admissions Office; (3) activities aimed at improving the general climate for women at Montana Tech, particularly for those in the engineering disciplines; and (4) activities to prepare women students for professional employment.

The Access Project will use internal funds to continue the activities under the Women in the Engineering Curriculum, such as the Lecture Series, and to expand the scope of project-related activities. The establishment of a special collection of women's resources in the college library is also planned.

Project Director

Suzanne Weghorst, Director of Cooperative Education, Montana Tech, Butte, MT 59701.

Weber State College
Expanding Options for Women Students

Institutional Background

Weber State College is a four-year state-supported institution with an undergraduate enrollment of 10,000 students and a small Master of Education program. The student body is 43 percent female; and women make up one-fourth of the full-time faculty.

At Weber State, support for faculty development is expressed in a generous budget for the Office of Instructional Development, which administers a fund for faculty projects aimed at instructional improvement and curriculum development. This fund, along with matching funds from the Office of Grants and Contracts, provided additional monies to the equity project, eventually tripling the resources available to carry out the project.

For several years a small group of faculty has worked toward development of a women's studies program. At present, a proposal exists for a concentration assembled from several existing courses. There is also a strong Women's Educational Resource Center which contributes significantly to the awareness of women's issues at the college and in the community.

Inception and Definition of Project

Women at Weber State College still elect to major in the "traditional" majors such as nursing and teaching. Thirty-seven percent of the women who graduated in 1981 majored in Allied Health and 19 percent in Education; only 1.7 percent majored in Natural Sciences.

Concern about the underrepresentation of women in science and mathematics prompted a group of faculty and administrators to respond to the Northern Rockies Program on Women in the Curriculum with a project plan designed to increase the participation of women in science. The project had four objectives: (1) to train faculty in selected departments to recognize sex bias in curricular materials and to develop new or revised materials free of bias; (2) to develop an advising system that encourages women to explore interests and talents in nontraditional fields; (3) to design and implement Science and Math Anxiety Clinics for students and instruct science and math faculty on how to help students who experience anxiety; and (4) to pilot test and seek funding for a speakers program to bring women working in nontraditional jobs into public school classrooms.

The project team consisted of a faculty member in Zoology (Project Director), the department head of Secondary Education, and the department head of Distributive Technology.

Plan of Action

To build support for the project, a broadly based advisory board was named that included the Deans of Education, Natural Sciences, and Student Affairs; the Assistant Vice President for Academic Support; Directors of the Women's Educational Resource Center, the Graduate Program in Education, Ethnic Studies, and the Office of Instructional Development; selected faculty members; a student from the School of Education; the Director of the Mountain West sex and Race Desegregation Assistance Center in Ogden; members of the local school board, school superintendents, and community members. The board provided important community visibility (including media coverage locally), identified resource people who could assist with the project activities, and suggested ways to implement project goals.

The recruitment of faculty to participate in project activities was an important consideration in project planning. The project team felt that there were many people who needed to be reached but that the best use of time and energy would be to serve those faculty members who were already concerned about the issues addressed by the project by increasing their knowledge and skills. Several activities were aimed at a general audience; all were announced to the entire faculty but no incentives other than self-edification were offered for participation.

A particular opportunity for faculty development presented itself in the School of Education, where a review of the Teacher Education Program was under way. The Dean of the School was approached and lent his support to the project by encouraging faculty to attend a seminar on sex bias in instructional materials. An application for matching funds was submitted to and funded by the Office of Instructional Development.

The Education workshop, conducted in May 1982 by the staff of the Sex and Race Desegregation Assistance Center, provided the faculty with an overview of the nature and extent of bias in instructional materials and methods for alleviating it. Suggestions were made for revising "WILKITS" (Weber Individualized Learning Kits used for self-paced instruction) to eliminate bias and incorporate material on the experience and contributions of women in the field of education.

The project team worked with the staffs of the Women's Educational Resource Center, the Counseling and Academic Advisement Center, and the Sex and Race Desegregation Assistance Center to design and implement faculty workshops on improving advising skills. Topics included advising nontraditional students, listening skills, and learning anxiety.

Project matching funds from the Office of Grants and Contracts provided the opportunity to invite Jeffry Mallow and Sharon Greenburg from Loyola University to conduct a faculty workshop on science anxiety and advise faculty on how to set up a Science Anxiety Clinic. Thirty-five faculty from the sciences, mathematics, and the Counseling Center attended; several local public school teachers also attended. The result of the workshop was the establishment of Science Anxiety Clinics in the Counseling Center, run jointly by a counselor and a faculty member from one of the scientific disciplines.

Several project activities were directed toward the public schools. The Utah Math/Science Network was contacted and efforts to design and implement a Speakers Program at WSC were merged with their efforts to provide an expanded list of potential speakers. Several of the faculty members at Weber State also participated in the Math/Science Network Conference "Expanding Your Horizons," held in February of 1983. In addition, awards were presented at the regional high school science fair to six "Young Women Scientists of the Year" for their projects. An award recipient was chosen for each of the six grades represented at the fair.

Other project activities included a presentation to the faculty by the Director of the Sex and Race Desegregation Assistance Center on gender bias in advertising; a faculty seminar entitled "A Woman's Place is in the Curriculum"; a workshop for students in the School of Education on science anxiety and its effects on school children; and a faculty workshop on classroom gender bias.

Short-Term Impact

The impact of the project on the faculty varied tremendously depending on the individual faculty member's level of participation in project activities. Many who participated regularly have made course revisions designed to eliminate gender bias. The attendance at the workshops and seminars was generally in the range of eight to twelve, with the exception of the School of Education workshops on gender bias and science anxiety (about twenty-five participants) and the Mallow/Greenburg Science Anxiety workshop (about thirty-five participants). The students involved in the Science Anxiety Clinics experienced significant reductions in anxiety and increased skill in identifying their anxiety and developing necessary coping behaviors.

Future Activities

Additional funding is available from the Instructional Development grant to support future workshops on curricular bias in the Schools of Technology and Natural Sciences. The Science Anxiety Clinics are currently being revised and will become part of a larger program of the Counseling/Academic Advisement Center to address learning anxiety in a number of areas. The Mallow/Greenburg videotape is being edited and made available as a resource to the other schools who participated in the project. Cooperation with the Utah Math/Science Network also resulted in the planned expansion of the "Expanding Your Horizons" Conference to include participants from more northern parts of the Wasatch Front area. Another workshop for public school cooperating teachers is planned to address the problem of science anxiety and its effects on school children. And, the Young Woman Scientist of the Year awards will continue to be offered at the regional high school science fairs.

Project Director

Gloria Wurst, Department of Zoology—2505, Weber State College, Ogden, UT 84408.

7

Directory of Projects

This directory of projects is an edited listing of the projects included in the 1984 *Directory of Projects: Transforming the Liberal Arts Curriculum through Incorporation of the New Scholarship on Women*, compiled by Barbara Kneubuhl and Peggy McIntosh of the Wellesley College Center for Research on Women under a grant from the Andrew W. Mellon Foundation. The Wellesley *Directory* was compiled in April 1984; the final *Directory of Projects* to be produced under the current Mellon Foundation grant will be available in spring 1985. The *Directory* has been augmented here by the addition of twenty-one newer projects funded by the Western States Project on Women in the Curriculum (see annotation under **Southwest Institute for Research on Women**). These projects are specifically identified as belonging to the Western States Project.

This directory is provided here to convey a sense of the breadth of the movement to incorporate the new scholarship into the curriculum and of the variety of institutional settings and curricular change strategies within the movement. While the settings and curricular change strategies vary, these projects do share a common aim, as described in the Preface to the original Wellesley *Directory*: "to help faculty in traditional disciplines to use the key research findings and transforming insights which may arise from feminist studies to develop new perspectives on their work as teachers and scholars" and "to secure and strengthen Women's Studies programs."

This listing of projects has been edited to eliminate duplication and to update a few entries where new information was available. Not included are the annotations for projects described in detail in other sections of this book. References to items in the bibliography have been substituted for the descriptions and contact information in the annotations of those projects designed to produce or disseminate new curriculum materials. Ordering information for materials produced by campus-based projects has also been replaced by references to the bibliography. Finally, references to articles in the bibliography that describe various projects have been added to the annotations.

Abbreviations used in this directory include:
FIPSE: Fund for the Improvement of Postsecondary Education
NEH: National Endowment for the Humanities
WEEAP: Women's Educational Equity Act Program

Alverno College
Greta Salem, Department of Social Science and Policy Studies, Alverno College, 3401 South 39 Street, Milwaukee, WI 53215

As well as undertaking a systematic redefinition of the curriculum in the Department of Social Science and Policy Studies, Alverno is also engaged in an effort to bring women's studies materials into all disciplines: it runs a faculty institute three times a year, part of which is devoted to women's issues under the direction of the Research Center on Women; and a faculty group, chaired by the academic dean, is actively encouraging teaching about women. This is an innovative program at a small, committed college.

American Historical Association

A Ford Foundation grant enabled the Committee of Women Historians of the AHA to produce "Teaching Women's History," an eighty-eight-page booklet written by Gerda Lerner, Professor of History at the University of Wisconsin, Madison. See #104.

American Political Science Association

The APSA Task Force on Women and American Government, chaired by Diane Fowlkes (see Georgia State University), has developed nine curriculum units for incorporation into American Government courses under the general title *Citizenship and Change: Women and American Politics*. See #112.

American Psychological Association
Nancy Felipe Russo, Administrative Officer, Women's Programs, APA, 1200 17 Street, NW, Washington, DC 20036

The Women's Programs Office of the APA serves as a catalyst for the production of materials that can be used in psychology courses on sex roles and on the psychology of women. See #114. *Sex and Gender in the Social Sciences: Reassessing the Introductory Course. Introductory Psychology*, by Judith M. Gappa and Janice Pearce, is available (#115).

American Sociological Association

The ASA publishes and distributes *Sex and Gender in the Social Sciences: Reassessing the Introductory Course. Introductory Sociology*, a teaching instrument developed by Judith M. Gappa and Janice Pearce (see Utah State University), with Barrie Thorne of Michigan State University as major contributing author. See #119.

Association of American Geographers

This organization has sponsored the production of a book, *Women and Spatial Change: Learning Resources for Social Science Courses*, edited by Arlene Rengert and Janice Monk (University of Arizona). See #101.

Bennett College

Helen Trobian, Director, Interdisciplinary Studies Program, Bennett College, Greensboro, NC 27420

Faculty are developing a curriculum module, "Gender Difference and the Development of Moral Judgment," funded by a small Mellon grant, to be used in interdisciplinary studies to focus on the inclusion of women in research on moral issues. The module includes a gender-oriented bibliography. Two handbooks, "Bioethics and Research" and "Sex Equality and Religion," prepared by Ruth Lucier and Helen Trobian, are available at cost for philosophy, religion, and interdisciplinary courses to generate class discussion and awareness of these issues.

Carleton College

Jane McDonnell, Coordinator, Women's Studies Program, Carleton College, Northfield, MN 55057

With a two-year grant from FIPSE, a project on new feminist scholarship and the curriculum enables faculty to develop the core of an innovative concentration in women's studies, consisting of four new courses. These include three "critique" courses (in anthropology, literature, and philosophy) which deal with current theoretical scholarship on women and gender, and a final "topics" seminar on racism and sexism. The project is sponsoring a women's studies lecture series and a series of faculty re-training seminars in spring 1984, led by outside scholar-consultants in diverse fields. A two-day symposium in fall 1984 concluded the project.

Central Washington University

Dorothy Sheldon, Director, Center for Women's Studies, Central Washington University, Ellensburg, WA 98926

A general faculty workshop on women's studies scholarship was held from which a core group of six faculty was selected to attend a year-long seminar series and revise courses in the general education curriculum. Funded by the Western States Project on Women in the Curriculum.

Claremont Colleges (Scripps, Pitzer, Pomona, Claremont McKenna, and Harvey Mudd)

Susan Seymour, Women's Studies Coordinator of the Claremont Colleges, Balch 21, Scripps College, Claremont, CA 91711

Scripps College is the center of activity for faculty and curriculum development in women's studies within this consortium of five small and very independent liberal arts colleges. With a Mellon faculty development grant, the Women's Studies Field Committee sponsored a conference, "Traditions and Transitions: Women's Studies and a

Balanced Curriculum," in 1983 at Claremont. Its aim was to encourage and support the reorganization and development of courses that focus on or include the new research on women and gender. The Committee also seeks to influence college hiring and curriculum policies by organizing faculty seminars and colloquia focusing on research on women. The 1984 faculty development seminar series, held at Scripps, involved interdisciplinary study groups working on a wide range of topics. These included: differences of race, ethnicity, class, and sexual identity; economic and political perspectives on women and poverty; feminist theory; adolescent development; and more discipline-centered inquiries on women and gender issues in science and mathematics, history, literature, and the arts. An excellent bibliography and three talks prepared for the 1983 Conference are available (see #152).

Colby-Sawyer College
Nancy Jay Crumbine, Coordinator, Women's Studies Program, Colby-Sawyer College, New London, NH 03257

The faculty of the College, in setting up a core curriculum consisting of five interdisciplinary courses and a selection of core electives, has committed itself to the integration of the new research on women into these courses. A two-day faculty development workshop in December 1983 provided the incentive for syllabus re-design work in the humanities and social sciences. The Humanities Department will pilot a core course in fall 1984, and the Social Sciences core will be introduced in 1985–86. A subcommittee of the Curriculum and Instruction Committee is advising and overseeing departments as these courses are developed and implemented.

College of St. Mary
Elizabeth Mulliken, Director of Faculty Development, Office of the Vice President for Academic Affairs, College of St. Mary, 1901 South 72 Street, Omaha, NE 68124

This project aims to increase faculty awareness of the new scholarship on women through an all-faculty workshop and review of discipline-specific materials and to initiate revision of general education courses. Funded by the Western States Project on Women in the Curriculum.

Colorado College
Margaret Duncombe, Department of Sociology, Colorado College, Colorado Springs, CO 80903

A series of seven general faculty seminars with outside consultants in women's studies will be held to review the new scholarship on women and to apply it to the revision of selected courses. Funded by the Western States Project on Women in the Curriculum.

Colorado State University
Mary Boland, Department of Social Work, 210 Eddy Building, Colorado State University, Fort Collins, CO 80523

An interdisciplinary team of curriculum consultants will identify areas of the professional social work curriculum for revision and design and implement a faculty development workshop to revise core undergraduate and graduate courses in the department. Funded by the Western States Project on Women in the Curriculum.

Dartmouth College
Anne Brooks, Coordinator, Women's Studies Program, Dartmouth College, Hanover, NH 03755

The Women's Studies Program, co-chaired by Mary Jean Green and Brenda Silver, provides inservice training to faculty in other disciplines and supports a variety of outreach projects specifically aimed at faculty development. With funds from the Leadership in Educational Equity Project (see **University of Maine at Orono**) and the College administration, the Program sponsored in 1983 a very successful conference on feminist scholarship as well as a faculty development seminar on Third World women. Both events have led to the revision of established courses and the creation of new courses. An important focus for faculty and curriculum development activity in 1984 has been women, gender, and science. Two woman-centered courses in the biological sciences are being offered as a result of the work. A report on integrating women into the curriculum, recently prepared by the Women's Studies Program, provides detailed information on the outreach projects.

Denison University
Margot Duley-Morrow, Coordinator, Women's Studies Program, Denison University, Granville, OH 43023

A five-year Mellon award (to 1983) supported faculty development activities leading to the formation of a faculty group of academic and career advisors for women students. The network of faculty advisors represents departments in which women students are commonly underenrolled—mathematics and computer science, economics and political science, the natural and physical sciences. New and revised courses, especially in mathematics, were also outcomes of the project. A final report is available. Denison has institutionalized its commitment to women's studies by requiring all students to take a course in minority or women's studies in order to graduate.

Duke University/University of North Carolina
Women's Studies Research Center
William Chafe, Academic Director; *Sandra Morgen*, Project
Director; Duke—UNC Women's Studies Research Center, 105 East
Duke Building, Durham, NC 27708

With a recent grant from the Rockefeller Foundation, the Center
is inaugurating a two-year curriculum transformation project designed
to change the ways in which English, social science, and history are
taught in colleges and high schools in North Carolina. The project is
intended to broaden the community of women's studies scholars and
to provide a model for joining the resources of secondary schools, colleges, and research universities to translate the lessons of the new
scholarship on women into basic curricular change. In addition, the
Center will award curriculum development grants in 1984-85 that are
intended to support college teachers to incorporate materials and perspectives on women into traditional courses or to develop courses in
women's studies. The awards are available to teachers in North and
South Carolina and Virginia. The Center issues a newsletter in the fall
and spring, and is disseminating materials from two faculty development events that it cosponsored in 1983, most notably a conference
report on "Equity and Excellence: Women's Studies and the Humanities" (see #48), and a bibliography prepared for the conference on
"Common Differences Between Black and White Women."

Earlham College
Cathy Milar, Department of Psychology, Earlham College,
Richmond, IN 47374

Earlham holds annual two-day faculty development retreats in
which the entire faculty participates. In 1984, in response to a plan
proposed at the Ninth Annual Conference of the Great Lakes Colleges
Association, of which Earlham is a member, the retreat focused on the
incorporation of women's studies into the main curriculum. The meeting, with outside speakers giving presentations and leading discussions and small group workshops, centered on curriculum integration
efforts in three broad areas: the humanities, social sciences, and
sciences. There was also a workshop devoted to the implications of
women's studies for administrative structures and policies.

Eastern New Mexico University
Janet O. Frost, Women's Studies Committee, Eastern New Mexico
University, Portales, NM 88130

Revision of courses in business administration, composition, history, and psychology will inaugurate a university-wide project to incorporate the new scholarship on women into introductory courses

with large and diverse student enrollment. Funded by the Western States Project on Women in the Curriculum.

Eastern Washington University
Gertrude (Lee) Swedberg, Director of Women's Programs, 115 Monroe Hall, Eastern Washington University, Cheney, WA 99004

Fourteen teams composed of a faculty member and a student research assistant integrated women's scholarship into twenty-three courses in twelve different academic areas. Funded by the Western States Project on Women in the Curriculum.

Evergreen State College at Vancouver
Virginia Grant Darney, Coordinator, Community Studies Program, Evergreen State College, 1002 East Evergreen Boulevard, Vancouver, WA 98661

This upper-division, interdisciplinary program integrates material by and about women into the core curriculum and emphasizes research methods. Disciplines include history, literature, political theory, and the social sciences. Weekly seminars for participating faculty focus on women's studies research and pedagogy.

The Feminist Press
Paul Lauter, Project Director, Reconstructing American Literature, The Feminist Press, Box 334, Old Westbury, NY 11568

An educational project of The Feminist Press supported by FIPSE, the project represented an effort to transform the teaching and thus the canon of American literature in response to the last two decades of work in women's and minority or ethnic studies. The project collected and published syllabi and other materials of changed courses as models, under the title *Reconstructing American Literature* (see ##109, 198).

Georgia State University
Charlotte McClure, Department of English, *Diane L. Fowlkes,* Department of Political Science, Project Co-directors, Georgia State University, Atlanta, GA 30303

A publication entitled *Feminist Visions: Toward a Transformation of the Liberal Arts Curriculum* is available (#31). It includes fourteen essays stemming from a very successful conference of scholars from eleven southern states, held in 1981 and entitled "A Fabric of Our Own Making: Southern Scholars on Women." The project has also developed two options for a concentration in women's studies, which lead to the B.A. in Interdisciplinary Studies, as part of an ongoing effort to balance the liberal arts curriculum through incorporation of materials on women. Funds for the project were provided by WEEAP.

Gonzaga University
Eloise Buker, Assistant Professor, Department of Political Science, Gonzaga University, Spokane, WA 99258

The Women's Studies Committee conducted a one-day workshop featuring a feminist scholar who introduced Arts and Science faculty to the new research on women and worked with selected faculty to integrate material into their courses. Funded by the Western States Project on Women in the Curriculum.

Great Lakes Colleges Association (Albion, Antioch, Denison, DePauw, Earlham, Hope, Kalamazoo, Kenyon, Oberlin, Ohio Wesleyan, Wabash, and Wooster)
Women's Studies Program: Katherine Loring, Coordinator, 220 Collingwood, Suite 240, Ann Arbor, MI 48103

The GLCA Women's Studies Program offers various faculty development activities for its twelve member colleges, emphasizing sharing and coordination of resources and information. The Program holds an annual conference focusing on women's studies curriculum development, revision of the standard curriculum, and issues of race, class, and sex as they affect dimensions of academic life and work. Proceedings of each annual conference are available (see ##42, 51–54), as is a newsletter. The Tenth Annual Conference took place at the Geneva Conference Center, Rochester, Indiana, on November 9–11, 1984. See also #66.

Guilford College
Carol Stoneburner, Director of Faculty Development, Coordinator of Women's Studies, Guilford College, Greensboro, NC 27410

A well-established faculty development program, supported by the College, encourages faculty members to take an interdisciplinary approach in designing courses that integrate material about women into the liberal arts curriculum. The Program sponsors activities that include faculty study groups, conferences featuring outside speakers, and workshops led by outside consultants. The study groups have been most effective in sustaining faculty interest in women's studies by providing a framework for informal discussion of specific topics, issues, and works of scholarship. See #67.

Harvard Divinity School
Constance Buchanan, Director, Women's Programs, Harvard Divinity School, 45 Francis Avenue, Cambridge, MA 02138

The Women's Studies in Religion Program, now ten years old, has, since its inception, fostered feminist scholarship with a view to transforming the study and practice of theology and the whole theological curriculum at the School. Ongoing support from the Ford Foundation and a recent grant from the Rockefeller Foundation have allowed the Program to reinforce and enlarge its mission by inviting research associates to develop materials that augment present course offerings, to teach, and to lecture in large forums on their work. The success of the research associates program was an important factor in the School's plan, initiated in 1979, to integrate feminist theology into its core curriculum. The recent Rockefeller award promotes new interdisciplinary approaches to the ongoing feminist inquiry and revision of courses by bringing to the School scholars from other humanities disciplines to do research and teaching.

Heritage College
Mary Carmen Cruz, Director, Individual Learning Center, Route 3, Box 3540, Heritage College, Toppenish, WA 98948
Selected faculty and staff participated in a two-day workshop about the new scholarship on women and developed and disseminated new bibliographies and syllabi. Funded by the Western States Project on Women in the Curriculum.

Hunter College/City University of New York
Susan Lees, Administrative Coordinator, Department of Anthropology, Hunter College/CUNY, 695 Park Avenue, New York, NY 10021
A two-semester curriculum change project in 1983 involved faculty from twenty-six departments in weekly workshops examining introductory survey courses with a view to including new research on women. The spring series included thirteen departments in the social sciences, mathematics, and sciences, and the fall series, an additional thirteen departments in the arts and humanities and education. A lecture series featuring outside speakers was held in conjunction with the workshops. Revised course materials and a report on the project are being prepared for dissemination.

Indiana University
Christie Pope, Director, Women's Studies Program, Memorial Hall East 128, Indiana University, Bloomington, IN 47405
A two-year curriculum development award from NEH has led to revision of the large introductory courses in Arts and Sciences at the University, and has resulted in the production of new course materials and a report entitled "Integrating Women's Studies Into the Curric-

ulum." Co-directors Barbara Hanawalt, Department of History, and
Jean Robinson, Department of Political Science, designed a project in
which women's studies faculty acted as mentors to professors who
received summer stipends to incorporate material on women into
courses whose combined enrollment is 9,000 students. Selected project materials and the final report were available in 1984 from the
Women's Studies Program. The Women's Studies Program also provides a bibliographic research service to Bloomington faculty who
want to integrate feminist scholarship into their courses. See #67.

Kansas State University
Sandra Coyner, Director, Women's Studies Program, Eisenhower
Hall, Kansas State University, Manhattan, KS 66506
     With an internal grant, a mainstreaming project is underway in-
volving four departments actively engaged in curriculum development. The project includes ongoing small-group, department-based
meetings and a general meeting of all participants each semester. History faculty are revising the introductory survey courses while, in Psychology, a new textbook has been developed and significant course
revision has taken place. The Education Department's work turns on
teacher behavior in the classroom, and Sociology has revised and developed new syllabi. The Program held a very successful statewide
conference last year on "New Humanities Scholarship on Women"
with funds from the Kansas Committee for the Humanities. Twenty
scholars were sponsored for the five-day event. See #68.

Cornelia Flora, Sociology, Anthropology, and Social Work, Waters
Hall 204, Kansas State University, Manhattan, KS 66506
     An ongoing seminar series for sociology faculty and graduate as-
sistants will be instituted for the purpose of studying and incorporating scholarship on women into basic sociology service courses.
Funded by the Western States Project on Women in the Curriculum.

Lewis and Clark College
Jean Ward, Assistant Dean of Faculty, Lewis and Clark College,
Portland, OR 97219
     A faculty development seminar in women's studies, funded by
NEH, was held in 1981 to promote gender-balancing the curriculum
by helping faculty to integrate materials on women into the core
courses of the College. Now, a very active Women's Issues Group
sponsors many gender-related projects: a women's studies symposium for faculty and students; a fall faculty retreat on mainstreaming
women's issues into the curriculum; and a task force to examine college publications for gender bias. A working paper on "The Issue of
Gender in the Lewis and Clark Curriculum" is available (#25) as well

as a model set of evaluation instruments, covering the entire cycle of the faculty development project. See also ##22, 24.

Lewis and Clark will host a Women's Studies Symposium to explore the integration of the new scholarship on women in math and science curricula and to disseminate to a regional audience results of the college's four-year effort to gender-balance the College's curriculum. Funded by the Western States Project on Women in the Curriculum.

Mankato State University

Carolyn Shrewsbury, Department of Political Science, Box 7, Mankato State University, Mankato, MN 56001

A Bush Foundation grant to the State University in Minnesota has supported a variety of faculty development efforts in women's studies at Mankato State. Spearheading 1983–84 activities was a series of faculty development workshops on feminist pedagogy led by Carolyn Shrewsbury, former Chair of Women's Studies. The workshops included faculty at other schools in the State System (Moorhead State, for example) as well as in the University of Minnesota System (e.g., University of Minnesota-Duluth). A similar series of workshops is planned in 1984–85. These workshops on teaching and learning in the feminist classroom complement other projects in the System that have focused on course materials. Mankato State is funding the publication of a monograph resulting from the workshops. See #67.

Memphis State University Center for Research on Women

Bonnie Thornton Dill, Director, Center for Research on Women, Clement Hall, Memphis State University, Memphis, TN 38152

With funds from the Ford Foundation, the Center, in conjunction with the Inter-University Research Group on Gender and Race, sponsored a very successful Summer Institute on Teaching, Researching, and Writing About Women of Color in 1983, with fifty teachers and scholars from across the country attending. The Institute provided a variety of forums for study, dialog, and debate, including lectures, research groups, topic groups, films, and panel discussions. Black, Asian, and Latina women in the U.S. were the focus of comparative theoretical discussions on the intersection of gender and race. A follow-up evaluation is currently being conducted. The Center is in the process of expanding its Summer Institute model into a larger faculty and curriculum development project. Its priorities for curricular change include working class women in the South, and women of color across the country. A detailed report on the Institute is given in the November 1983 issue of the Center's *Newsletter* (Shirley Johnson-Jones, Editor). See #195.

Mills College
Helen Longino, Coordinator, Women's Studies Program, Mills College, Oakland, CA 94613

With strong support from the College, Mills faculty are working on a new academic plan in which women's studies and feminist scholarship are systematically addressed. A faculty-wide conference held last fall devoted a session to the incorporation of women's studies into distribution requirements and to integrating new feminist research into general courses. A related lecture series included faculty in science, literature, history, and the social sciences. This spring, a faculty development seminar is continuing to deal with these two topics. The events are organized by the Women's Studies Committee, which has administered the major since 1976. A report on the year's work will be drafted by the Women's Studies Coordinator.

Montana State University
Project on Women in the Curriculum: Betty Schmitz, Director, College of Letters and Science, Montana State University, Bozeman, MT 59717

See Part One, Section 1: "Studies in Change," and ##57, 59, 60, 67, 70.

Western States Project on Women in the Curriculum: Northwest Regional Office, Betty Schmitz, Director.

See project description under **Southwest Institute for Research on Women.**

Moorhead State University
Evelyn J. Swenson, Affirmative Action Officer; *Nancy Parlin*, Dean, Natural and Social Sciences; Moorhead State University, Moorhead, MN 56560

Curriculum development seminars, supported by the Comstock Fund of the Minneapolis Foundation, have been held at Moorhead State in the last two years. The four-week summer intensives have enabled faculty in the humanities, natural and social sciences, and professional fields to develop new course offerings and revise established courses to reflect and latest scholarship on women and ethnic minorities. Follow-up sessions during the academic year give participating faculty the opportunity to assess and discuss the new and modified courses as they are implemented.

Mount Holyoke College
Penny Gill, Department of Political Science, Mount Holyoke College, South Hadley, MA 01075

The Mount Holyoke Project on Gender in Context, funded by the

Donner Foundation, seeks to construct a new basis for the academic pursuit of women's studies by creating a common methodology for a new stage of research on women. Focusing on definitions of gender, the project turns upon the study of the uses of language, both as societies define women's experience and as women describe it. Seven faculty from the College, representing six disciplines in the humanities and social sciences, are each studying a specific problem of gender in social context. In addition, invited outside scholars participate in four-week summer research seminars. The project is establishing a set of methodologies which may serve as models for cross-cultural, supradisciplinary studies on women. Academic year seminars, held about once a month, provide a forum for ongoing, interdisciplinary exchange and include faculty in the Five College Consortium as well as outside scholars. The Brown University Pembroke Center for Research on Women and the Smith College Project on Women and Social Change are participants in the project and will help with dissemination. The project plans to produce edited volumes of papers coming out of the seminars.

Northern Illinois University
Marilyn B. Skinner, Coordinator, Women's Studies Program,
Wirtz House, Northern Illinois University, DeKalb, IL 60115

A three-year, University-funded faculty development project in women's studies began in spring 1984, jointly sponsored by the College of Liberal Arts and Sciences and the Women's Studies Program. Faculty in three departments, each chosen on the basis of its large undergraduate clientele for required introductory courses, will take part in workshops that explore important new research on women and gender, and facilitate course revision. The workshops combine research, curriculum design, and pedagogy. The pilot workshop, offered by the Department of English, is on the current renaissance of black women writers.

Old Dominion University
Nancy Topping Bazin, Director, Women's Studies Program, Old
Dominion University, Norfolk, VA 23508

The Women's Studies Program offers biannual faculty development conferences for area colleges and universities as well as programs for faculty in specific disciplines. In March 1983, the Program held an institute on "Making Women Visible in Teaching History." In October, it sponsored a conference on recent feminist scholarship and the process of curriculum change. In spring 1984, faculty in Biology and Nursing participated in a conference examining the biological sciences in terms of the new research on women and, in addition, the Program is sponsoring a conference on feminist scholarship and its change potential for the sciences, social sciences, and humanities. In each case, visiting consultants, well known for their work to change the liberal arts curriculum in view of the new scholarship on women, presented a public lecture and conducted an all-day workshop. The Program's current emphasis is on integrating Third World materials into the curriculum. See ##26, 27, 67.

Organization of American Historians
Curriculum Materials Development Project: Elizabeth Fox-Genovese, Director, Department of History, SUNY Binghamton, Binghamton, NY 13901; *Joan Hoff-Wilson*, Executive Secretary, Organization of American Historians, 112 North Bryan, Indiana University, Bloomington, IN 47401

Under a FIPSE, then a Lilly grant, the OAH sponsored the development of course materials for integrating material on women into introductory history courses, which were published in 1983. See ##105, 106.

Regis College
Alice Reich, Faculty Development Committee, Regis College, West 50 Avenue and Lowell Boulevard, Denver, CO 80221

A Fall Faculty Conference initiated a year-long coordinated set of activities to integrate scholarship on women into the core curriculum, including workshops on women's scholarship, production of a handbook on nonsexist language and teaching practices, and development of bibliographies. Funded by the Western States Project on Women in the Curriculum.

St. Olaf College
Susan Lindley, Director, Women's Studies Program, St. Olaf College, Northfield, MN 55057

An active Women's Studies Committee, made up of faculty who represent the various academic divisions on campus, seeks to strengthen the women's studies curriculum while, at the same time, holding faculty workshops and retreats that focus on the incorporation of women's studies scholarship into the main curriculum. A series of faculty development workshops in 1983, supported by outside grants, has served to increase the base of faculty commitment to women's studies and to stimulate curricular transformation.

Sixteen College Informal Coalition (Agnes Scott, Cedar Crest, Chatham, Goucher, Hollins, Hood, Mary Baldwin, Mills, Randolph-Macon, Salem, Skidmore, Scripps, Spelman, Sweet Briar, Wells, and Wheaton)

Inzer Byers, Department of History, Salem College, Winston-Salem, NC 27108

A conference on "Scholars and Women," held at the University of Maryland at College Park in 1981, brought together faculty and administrators from the coalition to share research on the new scholarship on women and explore strategies for curriculum integration. Proceedings of the Conference, "Women's Studies and the Curriculum," edited by Marianne Triplette, Department of Sociology at Salem College, were published in book form in 1983 (#63). The project was supported with funds from the Carnegie Corporation and the Ford Foundation.

Smith College
Curriculum Coordinators: Susan Van Dyne, Department of English; *Marilyn Schuster,* Department of French; Wright Hall, Smith College, Northampton, MA 01063

The Smith curriculum transformation Project provides a model for maximizing existing faculty resources and facilitating interdisciplinary teaching and learning within conventional academic structures. In the last three years, faculty members whose courses already included significant material on women have joined colleagues just beginning to explore new scholarship on women to create an interdisciplinary course cluster each spring. A lecture and discussion series is used to coordinate four established courses from separate departments around a theme central to the grouping: "Women and Power" in 1982, "Women: Image and Identity" in 1983, and "Culture Constructs the Female" in 1984. In the last two years, intensive five-week faculty seminars in the fall semester have augmented the in-service training and team-teaching opportunities of the course cluster. The first two years of the Smith curriculum project were sponsored by the Mellon-funded Project on Women and Social Change. Now successfully institutionalized, the project is overseen by a faculty Advisory Committee on the Study of Women, chaired in 1984 by Ruth Solie, Department of Music. The extensive project literature includes, most notably, a bibliography for integrating research on women's experience in the liberal arts curriculum (#171), syllabus re-design guidelines, and a working paper by Marilyn Schuster and Susan Van Dyne, entitled "Feminist Transformation of the Curriculum: The Changing Classroom, Changing the Institution" (#61).

Southwest Institute for Research on Women
Myra Dinnerstein, Director; *Janice Monk,* Executive Director; 269 Modern Languages, University of Arizona, Tucson, AZ 85721

In 1983, the Southwest Institute for Research on Women (SIROW) received funding from the Ford Foundation to establish the Western

States Project on Women in the Curriculum to support curriculum integration activities at four-year institutions in sixteen states. The Northwest Regional Office of the project, directed by Betty Schmitz (see contact address at **Montana State University**), serves the states of Idaho, Montana, North Dakota, Oregon, South Dakota, Washington, and Wyoming; the Southwest Regional Office, directed by Myra Dinnerstein at SIROW, serves Arizona, Colorado, Kansas, Nebraska, Nevada, New Mexico, Oklahoma, Texas, and Utah.

In 1983–84, the project made grants to institutions in two categories: those seeking to initiate new projects to incorporate new scholarship on women into the curriculum, and those seeking to sustain efforts already underway. The project also sponsored two regional conferences in 1984, one in conjunction with the Northwest Women's Studies Association Conference in Bellingham, Washington, in April, and one in conjunction with the Rocky Mountain Modern Language Association Meeting in El Paso, Texas, in October.

In 1984–85, the project is sponsoring a consultant grant program to provide matching funds for institutions to bring women's studies scholars to campus to assist in initiating curricular change efforts. The project is also publishing a collection of syllabi for integrated courses and a directory of consultants in the region (see **#184**).

With funding from the U.S. Department of Education, a three-year faculty development project, entitled "Integrating Women into International Studies," began July 1, 1984, co-directed by Janice Monk, and Joyce Nielsen of the University of Colorado at Boulder. The project involves twelve campuses in Arizona and Colorado. Through workshops, seminars, and individual research, faculty members work to revise courses and methodology in the humanities and social sciences, selected professional programs, and foreign languages to include material on women. The project is designed to conduct yearly statewide conferences, to develop a regional network of faculty and a pool of consultants with expertise in curriculum integration, and to publish both materials for its participants and reports directed to a wider audience. See also entry under **University of Arizona** and **#209**.

Speech Communication Association
In 1983, the Association published *Removing Bias: Guidelines for Student-Faculty Communication*, a faculty development guide produced by Mercilee M. Jenkins, et al., **#78**.

Spelman College
Beverly Guy-Sheftall, Project Director, Women's Center, Box 127, Spelman College, Atlanta, GA 30314
With a two-year curriculum development grant from the Ford Foundation, Spelman College has designed a project to incorporate

black women's studies into the curricula of selected colleges in the Southern region. The project seeks to address the regional and racial biases in women's studies as a discipline as well as in the general curriculum. Its aim is both to reconceptualize women's studies and to transform the larger curriculum. During the first grant year, Spelman is engaged in extensive faculty and curriculum development efforts which include research, seminars, and workshops. These efforts establish the framework for coordinating similar projects at Morehouse, Clark, Kennesaw, and Agnes Scott Colleges.

Stephens College
Jeanine Lindstrom Elliott, Director, Women's Studies Senior Colloquium Curriculum Project, Box 2134, Stephens College, Columbia, MO 65215

A faculty workshop on Women's Education, inaugurated with a grant from NEH, is now held each year with internal funding. The year-long workshops provide stipends to faculty members to revise introductory and required courses to incorporate materials and perspectives relevant to women and ethnic minorities. New degree requirements, implemented in 1982–83, include integration of materials on women in all courses that students take to meet the liberal education requirement, and a senior colloquium, required for all B.A. candidates, which turns on contemporary women's experience. A series of reports, curriculum revision documents, and working papers emerging from the workshops are available from the Project Director. A book, entitled *All of Us Are Present,* resulted from the Stephens College Symposium (#28). See also ##44, 68.

Texas A & M University
Elizabeth Maret, Women in Development, Texas A & M University, College Station, TX 77843

A project to integrate the new scholarship on women into core introductory courses in the College of Liberal Arts will be initiated through the training of a core group of faculty by outside consultants and through the planning of general faculty development seminars. Funded by the Western States Project on Women in the Curriculum.

Towson State University
Sara Coulter and **Elaine Hedges,** Project Directors, Women's Studies Program, Towson State University, Towson, MD 21204

With a three-year grant from FIPSE, a major curriculum reform project is underway at this University. The project involves over seventy faculty members in workshops where they study the new scholarship on women during the first year, revise courses the second year, and test and evaluate the new courses as they are being taught in the third year. Thirteen representative introductory survey courses in eight disciplines have been chosen for revision. Two conferences are planned in conjunction with the curriculum change work, one on pedagogy and the other on interdisciplinary study. The project will conclude with a third faculty development conference for secondary schools, colleges, and universities in the Baltimore area. This final event is aimed at disseminating results and launching pilot curricular reform efforts at neighboring institutions.

University of Albuquerque
Glenda Gray, Director, Core Curriculum Subcommittee, University of Albuquerque, St. Joseph Place NW, Albuquerque, NM 87140

A series of discipline-specific bibliographies will be compiled and distributed to faculty interested in the incorporation of work by and about women into core courses and courses in the honors program. Funded by the Western States Project on Women in the Curriculum.

University of Arizona
Myra Dinnerstein, Director, Women's Studies Program, University of Arizona, Tucson, AZ 84721

With funds from the National Endowment for the Humanities (to July 1985), a three-year project is working to change the content and the structure of curriculum to include materials and scholarship on women by the following means: by conducting a series of faculty development activities that will enable faculty of basic courses in many departments to develop materials on women; by extending women's studies to the graduate level by establishing four new graduate courses in sociology, anthropology, political science, and history; and by revising the undergraduate women's studies curriculum. By the end of the grant period, thirty faculty members will have participated in the project. Selected materials from the NEH Curriculum Integration Project and three related reports are available (see #30). See also the entry under **Southwest Institute for Research on Women** for new projects based at the University of Arizona; and **#70**.

University of Connecticut
Pat Miller, Director, Project for a Balanced Curriculum, Women's Studies Program Office, Box U-181, University of Connecticut, Storrs, CT 06268

The University is funding a project, begun fall 1983, which seeks to bring feminist perspectives and materials on women into the general curriculum. A series of faculty development workshops in spring 1984 involve faculty and teaching assistants in two target disciplines (freshman English, political science) and outside consultants who are experienced in curriculum change work. Course and resource materials from the project were shared with the faculty at a book fair in April 1984.

University of Delaware at Newark
Project Directors: Margaret Andersen, Women's Studies/Sociology; *Sandra Harding,* Philosophy/Women's Studies; Women's Studies Program, University of Delaware, Newark, DE 19716

Under a grant from the University Provost's Office, the Women's Studies Program will sponsor a faculty development project in 1984–85 designed to integrate research on women into the introductory curriculum in the social sciences across the University. Following a fall faculty retreat, ten faculty members will be chosen to take part in a workshop, led by the project directors, which will turn on the new women's studies scholarship in participants' disciplines. Courses revised in the context of the workshop will be offered in fall 1985. During that semester, each faculty participant will invite to campus a feminist scholar/consultant to give a lecture in class and a colloquium in the "home" department. The Women's Studies Program also sponsors two lecture series, open to the University community, which meet weekly during the academic year. The Research on Women series is now in its eighth year, while the Research on Racism series began in spring 1984, with funds from the University Center for Teaching Effectiveness.

University of Idaho/Washington State University
Susan Armitage, Director, Women's Studies Program, Washington State University, Pullman, WA 99164–4032

Corky Bush, Assistant Dean, Student Advisory Services, Women's Center, University of Idaho, Moscow, ID 83843
See description on page 84.

University of Illinois at Chicago Circle
Margaret Strobel, Director, Women's Studies Program, University of Illinois, P.O. Box 4348, Chicago, IL 60680

With an award from FIPSE, the Multicultural Women's Summer Institute, held July 1983 on the Chicago campus, brought together twenty-five faculty from colleges and universities across the country to discuss incorporating material on women of color into interdisciplinary courses on women. Sessions were devoted to research presentations and discussion, pedagogy, and model syllabus design. With part of the grant designated for dissemination activities, participants are currently organizing outreach efforts and implementing new courses or revising old ones at their respective institutions. They have developed curriculum guidelines, reading lists, and bibliographies which are available from the project director, at the above address.

University of Maine at Orono
JoAnn M. Fritsche, Director, *Deborah Pearlman*, Associate
Director, Equal Opportunity/Women's Development Programs, 251
Aubert Hall, Orono, ME 04469

The Women in the Curriculum Program has ongoing University
support to finance a variety of faculty development activities at Orono
which are basically structured around course revision and training
faculty to become competent in women's studies scholarship. With a
grant from WEEAP, the Leadership in Educational Equity Project was
established within the Program to assist feminist faculty and administrators in seven other colleges and universities in Maine and New
Hampshire to develop pilot curriculum integration projects at their
own institutions. The Program directors have prepared a manual entitled *Toward Excellence and Equity: The Scholarship of Women as a Catalyst for Change in the University*, which will be ready for distribution
in 1985. Its purpose is to help academic feminists with the political issues involved in developing institutional support for curriculum integration work. See #67.

University of Massachusetts at Amherst
Margo Culley, Department of English, Bartlett Hall, University of
Massachusetts, Amherst, MA 01003

Under the auspices of the Women's Studies Program at the
University of Massachusetts at Amherst and the Afro-American
Studies Program at Smith College, a FIPSE-funded black studies-
women's studies project, involving faculty of the five college area,
has developed resource materials and a team of consultants on curriculum development and multi-ethnic feminist studies. The aim of the
project, which ended in 1983, was to ensure that women's studies
courses are truly inclusive and that black studies includes feminist
scholarship and perspectives. Participants in the project's faculty development seminars now serve as resource people and consultants in
a number of disciplines. They have produced a book of courses, addressing issues of race, gender, and culture, which is an invaluable
guide to faculty engaged in curriculum change work. Information
about the book and names of consultants may be obtained from Margo
Culley or from Johnnella Butler, Chair of Afro-American Studies at
Smith, who were co-directors of the project. See #94.

University of Nebraska at Omaha
Harvey Leavitt, Department of English, University of Nebraska at
Omaha, Omaha, NE 68162

A two-semester freshman humanities sequence will be revised by means of released time for course coordinators, faculty research grants, library acquisitions, and interdisciplinary colloquia. Funded by the Western States Project on Women in the Curriculum.

University of New Mexico
Elizabeth Stefanics, Women's Studies Program, 233 Marron Hall, University of New Mexico, Albuquerque, NM 87140

This project provides library computer assistance in generating women's studies materials for integration into selected courses. Funded by the Western States Project on Women in the Curriculum.

University of North Carolina at Greensboro
Judith White, Director, Women's Resource Center, 214 Mossman Building, University of North Carolina, Greensboro, NC 27412–5001

"Equity and Excellence: A Conference on Women's Studies and the Humanities" was held in 1983 on the Greensboro campus and co-sponsored by University of North Carolina-Greensboro and the Duke/UNC Women's Studies Research Center. The conference was funded by the North Carolina Humanities Committee and the Z. Smith Reynolds Foundation which has provided a grant for faculty development in women's studies to the University. A Conference Report edited by Judith White and Sandra Morgen is available (#48). UNC-Greensboro is currently engaged in course revision with a view to integrating women's studies and black studies into the general curriculum and strengthening cross-cultural studies. Led by the Women's Resource Center, which is in the Division of Academic Affairs, the work is multidisciplinary in focus and involves tenured faculty and department heads in many fields collaborating with the Women's Studies, Black Studies, and International Studies Committees. Stipends and released time to faculty, research scholarships, and workshops are made possible by the Reynolds grant and strong internal support for the efforts. See #67.

University of North Dakota
Sherry O'Donnell, Department of English, University of North Dakota, Grand Forks, ND 58201

A Bush Foundation award to the Women's Equity Committee made possible a series of faculty workshops on integrating women's studies into the traditional curriculum in which twenty faculty members from six different colleges of the University participated. The result of the project is *Women's Scholarship: A Curriculum Handbook* (#93).

Sandra Donaldson, Director, Women Studies, Associate Professor of English, P.O. Box 8237, University of North Dakota, Grand Forks, ND 58202

Building on the two-year project conducted by the Women's Equity Committee, Women's Studies faculty will conduct workshops for faculty on classroom climate, pedagogy, and teaching methods, and develop and stage a performance exploring the effects of sexism, racism, and class bias. Funded by the Western States Project on Women in the Curriculum.

University of Texas at Arlington
Sheila Collins, Graduate School of Social Work, UTA Box 19129, University of Texas at Arlington, Arlington, TX 76019
In a one-day colloquium and teaching workshop sponsored by the Center for Women's Studies, faculty teaching the U.S. history survey were introduced to the materials *Restoring Women to History* created by the Organization of American Historians (see #105). Funded by the Western States Project on Women in the Curriculum.

University of Texas at El Paso
Kathleen Staudt, Women's Studies Program, University of Texas at El Paso, El Paso, TX 79968
A two-day workshop will be held for faculty who teach required first-year courses in English, history, and political science to assist them in preparing integrated syllabi. Funded by the Western States Project on Women in the Curriculum.

University of Utah
Ann Parsons, Department of English, 341 Orson Spencer Hall, University of Utah, Salt Lake City, UT 84112
The University Writing Program will add a strategic section and bibliography on gender to the instructional guide for introductory writing courses, conduct colloquia on gender balance for current teachers of writing, and create an orientation session for new writing teachers. Funded by the Western States Project on Women in the Curriculum.
See also the earlier project described on page 181.

University of Wisconsin at Green Bay
Estella Lauter, Associate Professor, Humanistic Studies and Literature and Language; *Jerrold Rodesch,* Associate Professor, Humanistic Studies and History; Department of Humanistic Studies, University of Wisconsin, Green Bay, WI 54301–7001
In 1982-83 the University began a balanced curriculum project that seeks to promote the inclusion of new research on women into introductory courses throughout the curriculum. The project has included meetings and discussion with faculty, distribution of course materials and bibliographies, faculty seminars on feminist scholarship, demonstration classes, and exchange visits with Wheaton College.

Demonstration classes, held in 1983 and 1984, and led by the project directors, are focused on the art history, history, and literature curricula. Since fall 1983, the project has sought to strengthen its institutional base, working closely with the Faculty Senate.

University of Wyoming
Janice Harris, Head of Honors Program, Department of English, Hoyt Hall; *Katherine Jensen,* Chair, Women's Studies Committee, Department of Sociology, Ross Hall, University of Wyoming, Laramie, WY 82071
See description on page 68.

Jean Schaefer, Associate Professor of Art History, College of Arts and Sciences, University of Wyoming, Laramie, WY 82071
As one phase in the University's effort to incorporate women's perspectives in the curriculum, a visiting scholar and a research assistant assisted faculty in the development of bibliographies and other course materials to integrate gender issues into an Honors-Scholars General Education course on Epistemology. Funded by the Western States Project on Women in the Curriculum.

Utah State University
Judith M. Gappa, Project Co-Director, Associate Provost, San Francisco State University, 1600 Holloway Avenue, N-AD 455, San Francisco, CA 94132; *Janice Pearce,* Project Co-Director, Department of HPER, Utah State University, Logan, UT 84322
A WEEAP project has resulted in the development of three guides for transforming introductory courses in psychology, sociology, and microeconomics, as well as guidelines on student-faculty communications. Entitled "Sex and Gender in the Social Sciences: Reassessing the Introductory Course," the project guides are being published and distributed by different organizations. For information on the psychology and sociology guides, see #115 and 119 respectively; for the student-faculty communications unit, see #78. For the microeconomics guide, see #96.

Wake Forest University
Margaret S. Smith, Chairwoman, Department of Art; *Susan H. Borwick,* Chairwoman, Department of Music; Women's Studies Committee, Box 6032, Wake Forest University, Winston-Salem, NC 27109
Two parallel strategies are being used at Wake Forest to establish women's studies in the liberal arts curriculum. The first is to develop the minor program by expanding the women's studies core curriculum; and the second is to incorporate materials and methods from

women's studies into established liberal arts course offerings. The introductory core course in women's studies, offered for the first time in spring 1984, was developed with a grant from the Duke-UNC Women's Studies Research Center. At the same time, a grant from the North Carolina Humanities Committee, matched by funds from the University, made possible a lecture series in which faculty participants from several humanities disciplines examined the relationships between women's studies and the main curriculum. The Women's Studies Committee has also planned a three-year project of summer seminars in women's studies in which thirty liberal arts faculty members will participate.

Wellesley College Center for Research on Women
Black Women's Studies Faculty and Curriculum Development Project: Margo E. Bradford, Coordinator, Center for Research on Women, Wellesley College, Wellesley, MA 02181

With a two-year grant from FIPSE, this project is developing a black women's studies concentration in collaboration with humanities and social sciences faculty from twelve historically black institutions. Using workshops held in May 1983 and January 1984 at Spelman College's newly established Women's Research and Resource Center, the project emphasized curricular reform study groups, resource sharing, and networking with a view to redesigning existing courses to include content on black women in the curriculum of these colleges and universities. Workshop participants and project staff have developed survey instruments to evaluate the project that will be used in writing the final report. Project directors are Patricia Bell Scott, Gloria T. Hull, and Barbara Smith, the co-editors of the important collection of essays, *But Some of Us Are Brave: Black Women's Studies* (#12). See also #194.

Faculty Development Program: Peggy McIntosh, Program Director, Center for Research on Women, Wellesley College, Wellesley, MA 02181

With a grant currently from the Mellon Foundation, this nine-year-old program fosters faculty and curriculum development in women's studies mainly in three ways. The National Consultant Program matches funds provided by college administrators to bring to their campuses outside consultants on women and the curriculum. The Regional Seminar Program gives stipends to New England area faculty to participate in Center-based interdisciplinary seminars dealing with the implications of feminist scholarship for the liberal arts disciplines. The National Fellowship Program offers grants for research and writing on disciplinary change. Science and technology are the seminar and fellowship focus in 1984–85. The Faculty Development Program also publishes an annual *Directory of Projects* (**#185**) and a *Directory of Consultants* (**#183**) in curriculum change work, issued three times a year.

Guidebook for Faculty and Curriculum Development: Peggy McIntosh, Center for Research on Women, Wellesley College, Wellesley, MA 02181; *Elizabeth Minnich,* 400 East Tremont, Charlotte, NC 28203

With a two-year grant from the Ford Foundation, the project co-directors are writing a book on the implications of women's studies scholarship and feminist pedagogy for the humanities. In preparing the book, the project staff are consulting on draft chapters with scholars in thirteen humanities disciplines and working with groups of faculty at four universities selected as sites for workshops to test and evaluate the chapters. The guidebook is intended primarily for an audience of college-level faculty both in women's studies and in the traditional disciplines. The project emphasizes a cooperative working model by involving many diverse scholar-consultants and, in the evaluation process, about sixty faculty participants in order to achieve a level of analysis and to develop a terminology accessible to a wide range of readers. Inquiries are welcome.

See also **#210**.

Western Washington University, Fairhaven College
Kathryn Anderson, Director of Women Studies, Fairhaven College, Western Washington University, Bellingham, WA 98225

The Fairhaven College faculty of fourteen will participate in a year-long seminar, beginning with a retreat in the fall and ending with a colloquium in the spring, to redesign seven required core courses from the perspective of equity in gender, race, and class. Funded by the Western States Project on Women in the Curriculum.

Western Wyoming College
Gayle Yamasaki, Coordinator, The Women's Center, Western Wyoming College, 2500 College Drive, Box 190, Rock Springs, WY 82901

See project description on page 71.

Wheaton College
Frances Maher, Department of Education, Wheaton College, Norton, MA 02766

"Toward a Balanced Curriculum: Integrating the Study of Women into the Liberal Arts," a three-year project, funded by FIPSE, aimed at changing introductory courses in all disciplines to include new scholarship on women, has become a model for many institutions doing similar work across the country. In June 1983, the project sponsored a national training conference, held for the purpose of disseminating results and assisting teams of educators from other schools to begin their own projects. The Proceedings of the Conference are entitled *Toward a Balanced Curriculum* (#62). In addition, selected project materials are available including evaluation instruments, project reports and the brochure, reading lists for faculty, and an annotated bibliography on scholarship on women in French literature. During the school year 1984–85, expansion of the curriculum reform process to explicitly include the experience of women of color, Third World, and working women is intended. A speakers' series and faculty workshops are planned. See also ##22, 66, 67, 70.

Yale University
Nancy F. Cott, Chair, Women's Studies Program, 5046 Yale Station, New Haven, CT 06520

"Strengthening Women's Studies at Yale" is a three-year project of curriculum development (1983–86) funded by the National Endowment for the Humanities. The Women's Studies Program has elicited proposals from more than twenty faculty members in twelve departments, each of whom will, with the aid of a summer stipend or research assistance, revise or design a course. The overall project takes a two-pronged approach: half of the faculty members involved will transform existing courses (in the main, introductory lecture courses) to incorporate women's studies scholarship and feminist perspectives; and half will design new courses focusing on women and gender issues, which will be cross-listed under the Women's Studies Program. The project attempts to reach the widest possible undergraduate audience with the gains of the new scholarship on women while at the same time increasing the offerings of the Women's Studies Program. See #68.

PART THREE

Bibliography and Resources

8

General Works

WOMEN'S STUDIES AND FEMINIST SCHOLARSHIP
These works represent a selected group of historical and current analyses of the development and growth of women's studies in higher education and recent individual articles and collections of theoretical essays presenting representative critiques of traditional disciplines and methods of inquiry.

1. Abel, Elizabeth, and Emily K. Abel, eds. *The Signs Reader: Women, Gender and Scholarship.* Chicago: University of Chicago Press, 1983.

A collection of representative articles from the first thirty issues of *Signs* (#138) selected to elucidate salient trends in feminist scholarship in the social sciences, humanities, and natural sciences since 1975. Articles were selected to accentuate the revisionary force of feminist scholarship; to call attention to biases of race, class, and sexual identity; and to represent diversity in methodology, subject matter, and political perspective.

2. Bowles, Gloria, and Renate Duelli Klein, eds. *Theories of Women's Studies.* Boston: Routledge and Kegan Paul, 1983.

A collection of essays written between 1979 and 1982 that explore the relationship of women's studies to the structure of knowledge and the methodologies for acquiring knowledge; originally published as two volumes by the Women's Studies Program of the University of California-Berkeley. Contains an introduction by the editors on the relationship to women's studies of projects to integrate women's studies into the curriculum; thirteen theoretical essays; and a selected, annotated bibliography.

3. Boxer, Marilyn J. "For and About Women: The Theory and Practice of Women's Studies in the United States." *Signs: Journal of Women in Culture and Society* 7, 3 (Spring 1982): 661–95.

A review essay that surveys the literature about women's studies as a field in American higher education since its inception: its history, political issues, theories, and structures. Issues analyzed include the relationship of academic feminism to the women's movement; the adaptation of feminist principles to the classroom; feminist attempts to transform curricula; racism and homophobia in academe and in women's studies; and the formulation of feminist methodology.

4. Bunch, Charlotte. "The Reform Tool Kit." In *Building Feminist Theory: Essays from Quest* (#14).

An article that presents criteria for evaluating which reforms are useful and under what conditions feminists should work for reform within current institutions.

5. Cruikshank, Margaret, ed. *Lesbian Studies: Present and Future*. Old Westbury, N.Y.: The Feminist Press, 1982.

A collection of essays that describe the origins, extent, and diversity of lesbian studies within academe; its characteristics, goals, and assumptions; and current teaching practices. Includes a section on resources, an index to lesbian periodicals, an appendix of sample syllabi from courses on lesbianism, and a bibliographical guide to books and articles for instructors designing courses on lesbianism.

6. Dill, Bonnie Thornton. "The Dialectics of Black Womanhood." **Signs** 4, 3 (Spring 1979): 543–55.

A paper that analyzes four major problems in the literature on Afro-American families: inadequate or misinterpreted historical data; skewed assumptions about the relationship of blacks to white society; different values of researcher and research subject; and the general confusion of class and culture. Also presents alternative notions of womanhood generated through emphasis on women's work in Afro-American culture.

7. Hoffmann, Leonore, and Deborah Rosenfelt, eds. *Teaching Women's Studies from a Regional Perspective*. New York: Modern Language Association, 1982.

A collection of essays and curriculum materials on (1) the significance of regional sources in women's studies and (2) the development, pedagogical strategies, and feminist implications of teaching a student-centered course using these sources. Includes sample curriculum materials, a selected bibliography, and regional resources for the South. Available from the MLA, 62 Fifth Avenue, New York, NY 10011.

8. Howe, Florence. "Feminist Scholarship: The Extent of the Revolution." *Change: The Magazine of Higher Learning* 14, 3 (April 1982): 12–20.

An overview of the growth and development of women's studies. Includes a listing of content areas for the new body of scholarship on women that can be considered the basic curriculum of women's studies programs.

9. Howe, Florence, ed. *Women and the Power to Change*. New York: McGraw-Hill, 1975.

A collection of four essays on how the women's movement has affected women's lives and how institutions will have to be transformed to accommodate these changes; includes "Toward a Woman-Centered University," by Adrienne Rich; "Inside the Clockwork of Male Careers," by Arlie Russell Hochschild; "A View from the Law School," by Aleta Wallace; and "Women and the Power to Change," by Howe.

10. Howe, Florence, and Paul Lauter. *The Impact of Women's Studies on the Campus and the Disciplines*. National Institute of Education Women's Studies Monograph Series. Washington, D.C.: U.S. Government Printing Office, 1980.

A study of the impact that women's studies programs have had on the institutions that house them and on academic professional associations. Based on a review of the literature evaluating the impact of women's studies and materials from 119 women's studies programs, 57 professional societies, women's caucuses, and commissions. Concludes with recommendations for future policy and research.

11. Hubbard, Ruth, Mary Sue Henifin, and Barbara Fried. *Women Look at Biology Looking at Women: A Collection of Feminist Critiques*. Cambridge, Mass.: Schenkman Publishing, 1979.

A collection of essays on the politics and language of science and how biased assumptions in biological theory have supported the view of women as inferior. Includes a study of bias in evolutionary theory by Hubbard, an essay on the language of sex and gender by Fried, and a bibliography on women, science, and health by Henifin.

12. Hull, Gloria T., Patricia Bell Scott, and Barbara Smith, eds. *All the Women are White, All the Blacks are Men, But Some of Us Are Brave: Black Women's Studies*. Old Westbury, N.Y.: The Feminist Press, 1982.

A collection of essays from the black feminist movement that document the potential of black women's studies as "a feminist, pro-woman perspective that acknowledges the reality of sexual oppression in the lives of Black women as well as oppression of race and class." Includes essays on the politics of black women's studies and black feminism; racism and women's studies; black women and the social sciences; health; education; spirituality; and black women's literature. Also includes bibliographies, course syllabi, and recommendations for the future of black women's studies.

13. Moraga, Cherríe, and Gloria Anzaldúa, eds. *This Bridge Called My Back: Writings by Radical Women of Color*. Foreword by Toni Cade Bambara. Watertown, Mass.: Persephone Press, 1981. 2d ed. New York: Kitchen Table Press, 1983.

An anthology of literary and political writings by women of color in the U.S. that explore the roots of both their cultural heritage and oppression. Organized into six areas of concern: the roots of radicalism; feminist political theory and its racial/cultural background; cultural, class, and sexuality differences among women of color; writing as a revolutionary tool; and visions of a Third World feminist culture. Includes a bibliography of works by and about Third World women in the U.S.

14. Quest Staff and Quest Book Committee. *Building Feminist Theory: Essays from Quest.* Foreword by Gloria Steinem. New York: Longman, 1981.

A collection of twenty-four essays from the first three volumes (1974–1977) of *Quest: A Feminist Quarterly* (#134) that represent "the works of a group of feminists who have spent most of the past decade thinking about...class divisions experienced by women... the varying realities of race and culture; redefining power and the polarized options allowed by the patriarchy; the politics of sexuality and spirituality; new forms of organizations, leadership, strategy, and communication; and...the integrity of the process of change as part of change itself"(Foreword).

15. Nelson, Elizabeth Ness, and Kathryn H. Brooks. *Women's Studies as a Catalyst for Faculty Development.* National Institute of Education Women's Studies Monograph Series. Washington, D.C.: U.S. Government Printing Office, 1980.

A study of the extent to which women's studies has been involved in faculty development activities. Sources used include faculty development literature published since 1975, information from women's studies programs in the United States, and *Seven Years Later: Women's Studies Programs in 1976*, by Florence Howe (#73). Provides recommendations for furthering of faculty development in women's studies.

16. Patraka, Vivian, and Louise A. Tilly, eds. *Feminist Re-Visions: What Has Been and Might Be.* Ann Arbor, Mich.: University of Michigan Women's Studies Program, 1983.

A book of essays that respond to the question: "How has the new scholarship on women...changed our concepts of gender and our ways of looking at women's lives?" Essays are divided into three parts: reconstructing narrative (traditional realism, minority women writers, feminist drama, feminist science fiction); rethinking analytical paradigms (ideology of gender, psychological constructs, feminist research methods); and reinterpreting educational and political change. Available from the Women's Studies Program, University of Michigan, 354 Lorch Hall, Ann Arbor, MI 48109.

17. *Radical Teacher* 17 (November 1980): Women's Studies Cluster.

A special issue exploring two directions of women's studies in the late seventies: an increase in the commitment to teaching, research, and theory about the lives and work of black women and the development of lesbian studies. Includes articles of both a theoretical and a practical nature.

18. Sherman, Julia A., and Evelyn Torton Beck, eds. *The Prism of Sex: Essays in the Sociology of Knowledge.* Madison: The University of Wisconsin Press, 1979.

A collection of essays responding to the question of "what our fields of knowledge would now be like if women had been present in numbers and positions equal to men." Fields discussed are literature, history, psychology, sociology, philosophy, and political science.

19. *Signs* 7, 3 (Spring 1982): Special Issue on Feminist Theory.

A special issue of essays that explore history, culture, social institutions, and language from a feminist perspective and contribute to the formulation of feminist theory and method. Contains essays by Catharine Mackinnon, Temma Kaplan, Zillah Eisenstein, Evelyn Fox Keller, Jean Bethke Elshtain, Jane Marcus, and Susan Griffin; a review essay by Marilyn Boxer (#3); and related book reviews.

20. Spender, Dale, ed. *Men's Studies Modified: The Impact of Feminism on the Academic Disciplines.* New York: Pergamon Press, 1981.

A collection of essays by an international group of contributors that examines how and why women have been excluded from the academic disciplines and explores the impact of the women's movement on the traditional curriculum. Includes essays on language, philosophy, history, sociology, anthropology, psychology, economics, media studies, education, law, medicine, biology, and science.

21. Westcott, Marcia. "Feminist Criticism of the Social Sciences." *Harvard Educational Review* 49, 4 (November 1979): 422–30.

An article that reviews contemporary feminist criticism of the content, methodology, and purpose of knowledge about women as defined and practiced by the social sciences; proposes feminist alternatives to conventional analyses of women's experience.

22. *Women's Studies International Forum* 7, 3 (1984): Special Issue on Strategies for Women's Studies in the 80s.

A collection of articles edited by Gloria Bowles that addresses central issues and strategies for women's studies in the 1980s, in particular the relationship to women's studies and the potential impact of the curriculum integration movement. Includes versions of four papers originally presented at the 1982 National Women's Studies Association Plenary Session on "Autonomy or Integration": on women's studies and ethnic studies by Johnnella Butler; on similarities and perceived differences between the two approaches by Peggy McIntosh and Elizabeth Minnich; on the Lewis and Clark College project by Susan Kirschner and Elizabeth Arch; and on feminism and the academy by Marian Lowe and Margaret Lowe Benston. Also includes a critique of curriculum integration by Mary Childers and one by Helene Wenzel and Saj-nicole Joni; a synthesis of the accomplishments of women's studies by Deborah Rosenfelt; a description of the Wheaton College project by Bonnie Spanier; and an analysis of strategies for change embedded in feminist critiques by Gloria Bowles.

CURRICULUM INTEGRATION
This grouping contains major books, articles, conference proceedings, and special periodical issues that address the issue of integrating feminist scholarship into the curriculum. Several sources on the status of women students are also included.

Books and Articles
23. Andersen, Margaret L. "Thinking About Women and Rethinking Sociology." Working Paper No. 113. Wellesley, Mass.: Wellesley College Center for Research on Women, 1983.

A paper that argues for the retention of many of the fundamental theoretical assumptions of the sociological perspective that are consistent with a feminist analysis while making the discipline "true to its claims." The paper identifies these fundamental assumptions, presents issues and problems with current practice and their parallels with other disciplines, and reviews current issues in feminist sociology.

24. Arch, Elizabeth C., and Susan E. Kirschner. "Gender-Balancing: A Case Study of Institutional Change." *Educational Record*, forthcoming.

An article that describes and analyzes the progress toward the establishment of "gender-balancing the curriculum" as an institutional priority at Lewis and Clark College (Oregon). Events treated include faculty development activities and women's studies symposia; the formation of a Women's Issues Group; the preparation and dissemination of a report for the faculty on "The Issue of Gender in the Lewis and Clark Curriculum" (#25); and the establishment of an official committee to oversee issues dealing with women.

25. Atkinson, Jane, and Susan Kirschner. "The Issue of Gender in the Lewis and Clark Curriculum." Unpublished paper. Portland, Oreg.: Lewis and Clark College, 1982.

A planning document written for the general faculty that presents rationales and strategies for "gender balancing" the college's curriculum. Available from Susan Kirschner, Department of English, Lewis and Clark College, Portland, OR 97219.

26. Bazin, Nancy Topping. "Expanding the Concept of Affirmative Action to Include the Curriculum." *Women's Studies Newsletter* 8, 4 (Fall/Winter 1980): 9–11.

An article that describes how the transformation of the traditional curriculum to include women and minorities was built into the mission statement of Old Dominion University and how this reform was implemented. Discusses strategies, results, and implications of this change.

27. Bazin, Nancy Topping. "Integrating Third World Women into the Women's Studies Curriculum." *Frontiers* 7, 2 (1983): 13–17.

An article describing how the author integrated Third World material and perspectives into four interdisciplinary women's studies courses at Old Dominion University: Women in a Changing World, Women's Spiritual Quest, Women and Power, and Mothers and Daughters.

28. Bender, Eleanor M., Bobbie Burk, and Nancy Walker. *All of Us Are Present*. Columbia, Mo.: James Madison Wood Research Institute, 1984.

A volume of essays based on major addresses and panels of the Stephens College Symposium "Women's Education: The Future," which addressed problems for women inherent in traditional education and presented strategies for change. Of particular interest are Elizabeth Minnich's analysis of bias in the traditional curriculum; Patricia Bell Scott's essay on education for women of color; and Jeanine Elliott's summary of the panel on curriculum. Available from James Madison Wood Research Institute, P.O. Box 2134, Stephens College, Columbia, MO 65201.

29. Briscoe, A.M., and S. M. Pfafflin. *Expanding the Role of Women in the Sciences.* Annals of the New York Academy of Sciences, vol. 323. New York: New York Academy of Sciences, 1979.

A collection of thirty-one papers from the Conference on Expanding the Role of Women in the Sciences, New York, March 1978; arranged by topics, including the current status of women in science; opportunities for professional advancement; and strategies for change. Includes articles on physics and astronomy; the geosciences; psychology; dentistry, medicine, and veterinary medicine; engineering; mathematics; and the biological sciences. Available from the New York Academy of Sciences, 2 East 63 Street, New York, NY 10021.

30. Dinnerstein, Myra, Sheryl R. O'Donnell, and Patricia MacCorquo-dale. *How to Integrate Women's Studies into the Traditional Curriculum*. Tucson, Ariz.: Southwest Institute for Research on Women, n.d.

A report based on the experiences of seventeen projects represented at the SIROW Workshop on Integrating Women's Studies into the Curriculum, Princeton, N.J., August, 1981. Includes recommendations for initiating and sustaining a project; project abstracts; and an annotated list of resources reprinted from *The Forum for Liberal Education* (#67).

31. Fowlkes, Diane L., and Charlotte S. McClure, eds. *Feminist Visions: Toward a Transformation of the Liberal Arts Curriculum*. University, Ala.: University of Alabama Press, 1984.

A collection of essays "designed primarily to provide substantive research for those scholar/teachers who are beginning or are continuing...to integrate the new scholarship on women into their courses and curricula." Includes an introductory chapter by the editors on their Southern regional model for "gender-balancing" the liberal arts curriculum; a keynote conference address by Catharine Stimpson on the new scholarship on women; and fourteen essays reassessing knowledge bases from a feminist perspective. Also includes a selected bibliography and an index.

32. Gardiner, Linda. "Can This Discipline Be Saved? Feminist Theory Challenges Mainstream Philosophy." Working Paper No. 118. Wellesley, Mass.: Wellesley College Center for Research on Women, 1983.

A paper that briefly addresses problems that arise in seeking to make the discipline of philosophy recognize women. Reviews efforts of feminist philosophers to change the discipline and identifies specific problems in changing the philosophy curriculum in colleges and universities. The analysis is confined to the Western philosophical tradition as taught in the United States and treats the areas of history of philosophy, theory of knowledge, metaphysics, logic, and value theory.

33. Gappa, Judith M. and Barbara S. Uehling. *Women in Academe: Steps to Greater Equality*. AAHE-ERIC Higher Education Research Report, No. 1. Washington, D.C.: American Association for Higher Education, 1979.

A review of selected research results and published commentary,

1970–1978, on barriers to women in higher education. Describes causes and effects of inequities and suggests ways to improve women's status in postsecondary institutions. Available from AAHE, One Dupont Circle, NW, Suite 600, Washington, DC 20036.

34. Gillespie-Woltemade, Nellice. "The Feminist Academy and Third World Women." *Toward a Feminist Transformation of the Academy.* Ann Arbor, Mich.: Great Lakes Colleges Association Women's Studies Program, 1980.

Text of a presentation addressing the question of how a feminist transformation of the academy relates to Third World women; delivered at the 1979 Great Lakes Colleges Association Women's Studies Conference. Includes a short bibliography of resource materials on Third World women.

35. Hallett, Judith P. "Classics and Women's Studies." Working Paper No. 119. Wellesley, Mass.: Wellesley College Center for Research on Women, 1983.

A paper that discusses the integration of women into the classics curriculum. Includes a definition of the content and scope of the field of classics; its basic assumptions and methods; and the problems associated with integrating women into the study of classical antiquity.

36. Howe, Florence. "Those We Still Don't Read." *College English* 43, 1 (January 1981): 12–15.

Essay suggesting that during the 1980s attempts should be made to include the works of women writers in general literature anthologies and as topics of general literature classes. Calls for the transformation of the literary curriculum and a revision of critical theory and literary history to make them "coeducational, multiracial, multiclass, and inclusive of lesbian writings."

37. Humphreys, Sheila M., ed. *Women and Minorities in Science: Strategies for Increasing Participation.* American Association for the Advancement of Science Selected Symposium, No. 66. Boulder, Colo.: Westview Press, 1982.

A collection of twelve papers from a symposium at the 1980 annual meeting of the American Association for the Advancement of Science that describe the components and impact of programs to increase the participation of women and minorities in science from elementary school through college. Contributors include Lucy Sells, Betty Vetter, Nancy Kreinberg, Lenore Blum, and Alma Lantz.

38. Jiménez, Marilyn. "Contrasting Portraits: Integrating Materials about Afro-Hispanic Women into the Traditional Curriculum." Working Paper No. 120. Wellesley, Mass.: Wellesley College Center for Research on Women, 1983.

A paper that exposes "racist and sexist assumptions embedded in the language and content of Hispanic literature" by contrasting images of black and white women in selected periods and works in Spanish, Portuguese, and Latin American literature. Argues for a pedagogical approach that "leads us to ask what more and what else lies behind the official discourse on women" and for teaching works by black women authors in the traditional curriculum.

39. Kampen, Natalie, and Elizabeth G. Grossman. "Feminism and Methodology: Dynamics of Change in the History of Art and Architecture." Working Paper No. 122. Wellesley, Mass.: Wellesley College Center for Research on Women, 1983.

A paper that discusses some of the traditional methods and assumptions of twentieth-century art history and their impact on the study of women. The analysis contains three parts: an introductory section on how traditional methods and assumptions in art history have served to exclude women, artists of non-Western cultures, and certain art forms; a brief history of changes in the discipline brought about by recent feminist art criticism; and a discussion of the problems raised and solved by feminist approaches to the history of modern architecture.

40. Klein, Susan S., ed. *Handbook for Achieving Sex Equity through Education.* Baltimore, Md.: Johns Hopkins University Press, 1984.

A volume of articles addressing strategies to achieve sex equity in and through education. Includes sections on the nature and value of sex equity; administrative strategies; general educational practices; strategies in content areas; strategies for specific populations; early education and postsecondary education; and recommendations for continued achievement.

41. Langland, Elizabeth, and Walter Gove, eds. *A Feminist Perspective in the Academy: The Difference It Makes.* Chicago: University of Chicago Press, 1981.

A series of lectures delivered at Vanderbilt University, 1980–81, addressing the question of the impact of feminism on scholarship and teaching in specific disciplines; originally appeared in the winter 1981 issue of *Soundings: An Interdisciplinary Journal.* Includes essays on literary criticism, theatre arts, religious studies, American history, political science, economics, anthropology, psychology, and sociology.

42. Loring, Katherine, ed. *Seeing Our Way Clear: Feminist Revision of the Academy.* Ann Arbor, Mich.: Great Lakes Colleges Association Women's Studies Program, 1983.

Proceedings of the eighth annual GLCA Women's Studies Conference, November 5-7, 1982. Contains keynote presentations by Peggy McIntosh, Mary Beth Edelson, and Barbara Zanotti; selected papers on topics in women's studies; and a panel discussion, "Being Sensible or Selling Out?," on topics related to the politics of feminism in the academy. See also ##51-54.

43. Lougee, Carolyn C. "Women, History and the Humanities: An Argument in Favor of the General Curriculum." *Women's Studies Quarterly* 9, 1 (Spring 1981): 4-7.

An article that describes the implementation of a new undergraduate general studies curriculum at Stanford University, whose centerpiece is a course in Western civilization; analyzes reasons that Western civilization courses have traditionally excluded women and discusses various strategies employed at Stanford and elsewhere for integrating the study of women into core humanities curricula. Also presents ideas for revitalizing and redefining the humanities as central to undergraduate education.

44. McCauley, Nancy. "Implementing the Goals of Women's Education in the Humanities at Stephens College. Final Narrative Report." Paper presented at the 21st Annual Meeting of the Midwest Modern Language Association, Indianapolis, Ind., November 8-10, 1979.

A final report on the National Endowment for the Humanities demonstration grant, 1978-79, establishing women's studies at Stephens College (Columbia, Mo.); provides an overview of a model for faculty development and curricular change that focuses on women in the humanities. Includes nine papers on women in the humanities; course syllabi on women in the humanities; six departmental curricula on women's education; and goals of Stephens College for women's education. Available from ERIC Microfiche Services, #ED 185544.

45. McIntosh, Peggy. "Interactive Phases of Curricular Re-Vision: A Feminist Perspective." Working Paper No. 124. Wellesley, Mass.: Wellesley College Center for Research on Women, 1983.

A presentation that describes stages of perceptual and curricular revision that occur as one attempts to incorporate the study of women into a given discipline, and relates these stages to the hierarchical modes of thinking embodied in culture and society.

46. McIntosh, Peggy. "WARNING: The New Scholarship on Women May Be Hazardous to Your Ego." *Women's Studies Quarterly* 10, 1 (Spring 1982): 29-31.

An essay describing how the new scholarship on women transforms the traditional faculty member's sense of self.

47. McIntosh, Peggy. "The Study of Women: Implications for Reconstructing the Liberal Arts Disciplines." *Forum for Liberal Education* 4, 1 (October 1981): 1–3.

Brief overview of questions to ask as one attempts to reevaluate the traditional disciplines in light of the fact that women are more than half of the world's population.

48. Morgen, Sandra, and Judith White, eds. *Equity and Excellence: A Conference on Women's Studies and the Humanities.* Durham, N.C.: Duke—UNC Women's Studies Research Center, [1983].

A report of a conference on the impact of women's studies on the humanities held at the University of North Carolina-Greensboro, March 17–18, 1983. Includes keynote addresses on the humanities by Elizabeth Minnich, on Emily Dickinson by Elizabeth Phillips, and on anthropology by Karen Sacks; a series of reports on workshops on literature, history, black women's studies, anthropology, and women's studies; and a selected list of resources on curriculum transformation. Available from Duke—UNC Women's Studies Research Center, 105 East Duke Building, Durham, NC 27708.

49. Perun, Pamela J., ed. *The Undergraduate Woman: Issues in Educational Equity.* Lexington, Mass.: D.C. Heath, 1982.

A collection of seventeen papers on sex equity in education first presented at the Research Conference on Educational Environments and the Undergraduate Woman, Wellesley College, September 1979. Arranged in four sections dealing with historical and recent trends in college attendance by women; issues of access and selection in precollege years; issues of growth and change during college; and issues of outcomes and achievements during and after college.

50. Project on the Status and Education of Women. *Liberal Education and the New Scholarship on Women: Issues and Constraints in Institutional Change.* Washington, D.C.: Association of American Colleges, n.d.

A report of the 1981 Wingspread Conference on integrating women's studies into the liberal arts curriculum. Includes essays by Florence Howe on feminist scholarship (cf. #8), Elizabeth Minnich on the liberal arts, and Gerda Lerner on women's history, as well as the conference recommendations for institutions, administrators, faculty, and educational associations.

51. Reed, Beth, ed. *The Structure of Knowledge: A Feminist Perspective.* Ann Arbor, Mich.: Great Lakes Colleges Association Women's Studies Program, 1979.

Proceedings of the Fourth Annual Great Lakes College Association Women's Studies Conference, November 10–12, 1978. Includes a keynote address by Florence Howe on "Breaking the Disciplines," remarks from the opening panel on the structure of knowledge, and selected papers on topics in women's studies.

52. Reed, Beth, ed. *Toward a Feminist Transformation of the Academy.* Ann Arbor, Mich.: Great Lakes Colleges Association Women's Studies Program, 1980.

Proceedings of the Fifth Annual GLCA Women's Studies Conference, November 2–4, 1979. Includes a keynote address by Elizabeth Minnich, and presentations on feminism, curricular reform, Third World women, literature, and the arts.

53. Reed, Beth, ed. *Toward a Feminist Transformation of the Academy: II.* Ann Arbor, Mich.: Great Lakes Colleges Association Women's Studies Program, 1982.

Proceedings of the Sixth Annual GLCA Women's Studies Conference, November 7–9, 1980. Includes a keynote address by Elaine Reuben; selected papers on the implications of feminism for the disciplines and the academy; a paper on subject-heading access to works on women; and one on government publications for research on women.

54. Reed, Beth, ed. *Toward a Feminist Transformation of the Academy: III.* Ann Arbor, Mich.: Great Lakes Colleges Association Women's Studies Program, 1982.

The proceedings of the Seventh Annual GLCA Women's Studies Conference, November 6–8, 1981; includes papers on literature, critical issues in women's studies, and men in women's studies, as well as closing panel remarks on women's studies and the revision of liberal education.

55. Rich, Adrienne. "Taking Women Students Seriously." In *On Lies, Secrets, and Silence: Selected Prose, 1966–1978.* New York: W.W. Norton, 1979, pp. 237–45.

An essay (1978) that addresses teachers of women students, analyzes how women students experience "co-education," and discusses the implications of teaching women students. Offers recommendations for actively helping women students to identify and resist abusive situations.

56. Rochette-Ozzello, Yvonne. "Women's Studies and Foreign Language Teaching: A New Alliance." In *New Frontiers in Foreign Language Education, Selected Papers from the 1980 Central States Conference,* ed. Maurice W. Conner. Skokie, Ill.: National Textbook, 1980, pp. 35–48.

An essay connecting the pedagogy of teaching about women with that of teaching about a foreign culture. Includes suggestions for integrating the study of women into foreign language teaching and a selected bibliography on feminism, French feminism, and women in France. Also available from the Women's Studies Research Center, Reprint Series, No. 7, University of Wisconsin, Madison, WI 53706.

57. Schmitz, Betty, comp. *Sourcebook for Integrating the Study of Women into the Curriculum*. Bozeman, Mont.: Northwest Women's Studies Association, 1983.

A sourcebook in notebook format that contains sample materials from the ten projects participating in the Northern Rockies Program on Women in the Curriculum and selected other curriculum integration projects; divided into five sections on programs, sample materials, resources for faculty development, assessment materials, and bibliographies and additional resources. Includes the Wellesley College Center for Research on Women's 1983 *Directory of Projects* (**#185**); the *List of Non-Published Materials* from the Clearinghouse of Curriculum Integration Projects (**#170**); and the Schuster and Van Dyne bibliography (**#171**). Available from the author, College of Letters and Science, Montana State University, Bozeman, MT 59717.

58. Schmitz, Betty. "Women's Studies and Projects to Transform the Curriculum: A Current Status Report." *Women's Studies Quarterly* 11, 3 (Fall 1983): 17–19.

An overview of recent efforts to integrate women's studies into the curriculum and the relationship of this movement to women's studies; summarizes arguments for and against curriculum integration presented at the Wheaton College Conference "Moving Toward a Balanced Curriculum" (June 1983) and at the 1983 National Women's Studies Association Conference Plenary Session, "Envisioning the Future of Women's Studies: Autonomy/Integration/Transformation-/Revolution."

59. Schmitz, Betty, and Anne S. Williams. "Forming New Alliances for Women's Studies: The Northern Rockies Program on Women in the Curriculum." *Women's Studies Quarterly* 11, 1 (Spring 1983): 19–22.

General report on the inception and activities of ten curriculum integration projects in Idaho, Montana, Wyoming, and Utah; includes project abstracts.

60. Schmitz, Betty, and Anne S. Williams. "Seeking Women's Equity through Curricular Reform: Faculty Perceptions of an Experimental Project." *Journal of Higher Education* 54, 5 (September/October 1983): 556–65.

An article that describes a two-year project at Montana State University, 1979–81, to integrate content on women into the general curriculum; project implementation strategies, characteristics of faculty participants, faculty perceptions of project impact and student reaction, and barriers to the study of women in higher education are discussed.

61. Schuster, Marilyn R., and Susan R. Van Dyne. "Feminist Transformation of the Curriculum: The Changing Classroom, Changing the Institution." Working Paper No. 125. Wellesley, Mass.: Wellesley College Center for Research on Women, 1983.

A paper that describes pedagogical principles and internal dynamics of the "woman-centered classroom." The authors also identify and analyze the dynamics of models for institutional change that emerge from projects to integrate the study of women into the curriculum.

62. Spanier, Bonnie, Alexander Bloom, and Darlene Boroviak, eds. *Toward a Balanced Curriculum: A Sourcebook for Initiating Gender Integration Projects.* Cambridge, Mass.: Schenkman Publishing, 1983.

A sourcebook for initiating projects to integrate the study of women into the curriculum based on the Wheaton College Conference "Moving Toward a Balanced Curriculum," held June 22–24, 1983. Includes presentations on the relationship of gender integration to women's studies, on phases of curriculum integration, and on integration into the humanities, social, and natural sciences; discussions of institutional models at Smith, Wheaton, Montana State, and Yale; and presentations on political and pedagogical strategies for change and on locating resources. Also includes notes by Wheaton College faculty on revising courses in art history, biology, chemistry, education, English, history, music, political science, psychology, and sociology; bibliographies; descriptions of key resources; descriptions of discipline-based projects at Wheaton; and abstracts of the projects at the sixty schools in attendance at the conference.

63. Triplette, Marianne, ed. *Women's Studies and the Curriculum.* Winston-Salem, N.C.: Salem College, 1983.

Proceedings of a conference on "Scholars and Women," sponsored by Salem College at College Park, Maryland, March 13–15, 1981. Contents are divided into three parts: an overview of women's studies, with keynote addresses by Florence Howe and Catharine Stimpson; papers on research about women in the sciences, social sciences, and humanities; and articles about women's studies methodology, including "mainstreaming techniques" for courses in teacher education, sociology, literature, and philosophy. Available from Inzer Byers, Department of History, Salem College, Winston-Salem, NC 27108.

64. Wright, Barbara Drygulski. "Feminist Transformation of Foreign Language Instruction: Progress and Challenges." Working Paper No. 117. Wellesley, Mass.: Wellesley College Center for Research on Women, 1983.

A paper that traces and summarizes the evolution of a feminist perspective in foreign language instruction as it parallels the development of women's studies scholarship across the liberal arts. Three phases of development are considered: the focus on bias and sexism in foreign language textbooks; the concern with women's roles and status in the target culture; and the critical reevaluation of bias inherent in the target language itself and how that bias informs the teaching of the language. The critique incorporates positive ideas and suggestions for revising current practices in teaching foreign language and culture.

Special Periodical Issues

65. *Academe: Bulletin of the American Association of University Professors* 69, 5 (September/October 1983): Feminism in the Academy.

A special issue devoted to consideration of feminism's impact on the disciplines and the academy; features articles on literary criticism by Carolyn Heilbrun, on science by Evelyn Fox Keller, on economics by Barbara Bergmann, and on history by Carroll Smith-Rosenberg.

66. *Change: The Magazine of Higher Learning* 14, 3 (April 1982): Women's Studies at the University.

A special issue on women's studies and curriculum integration that includes, among others, essays on feminist scholarship by Florence Howe; on women's research centers by Mariam Chamberlain; on the program at Wheaton College by Bonnie Spanier; on the Great Lakes Colleges Consortium Women's Studies Program by Beth Reed; and on men in women's studies by John Schilb.

67. *The Forum for Liberal Education* 4, 1 (October 1981): The Study of Women in the Liberal Arts Curriculum.

Special issue of the *Forum* dedicated to the topic of integrating women's studies into the liberal arts. Includes an introductory essay by Peggy McIntosh on "The Study of Women: Implications for Restructuring the Liberal Arts Disciplines"; articles on programs at Wheaton College, Old Dominion University, Indiana University at Bloomington, the University of Maine at Orono, Mankato State University, Montana State University, Guilford College, and the

University of North Carolina at Greensboro; notes on eight additional programs; and an annotated resource list.

68. *The Forum for Liberal Education* 6, 5 (April 1984): The New Scholarship on Women.

A special issue that "describes the different ways colleges and universities are responding to the new scholarship on women." Includes an article by Peggy McIntosh on "The Study of Women: Processes of Personal and Curricular Re-Vision"; descriptions of programs at Yale, Smith, Kansas State, and Stephens College; program updates on seven of the institutions featured in the October 1981 issue of the *Forum* (#67); notes on programs at seven additional institutions; and an annotated resource list.

69. *Harvard Educational Review* 49, 4 (November 1979), and 50, 1 (February 1980): Women and Education.

A two-volume special issue of articles, essays, and book reviews devoted to assessing the impact of the women's movement on education and anticipating the future of women in education. Part I contains, among other articles, an introduction by Florence Howe on the first decade of women's studies; a feminist critique of the social sciences by Marcia Westcott (#21); and an analysis of "Woman's Place in Man's Life Cycle" by Carol Gilligan. Part II contains an article by Myra Sadker and David Sadker on "Sexism in Teacher Education Texts" (#87); and an update on math anxiety by Sheila Tobias and Carol Weissbrod.

70. *Women's Studies Quarterly* 10, 1 (Spring 1982): Transforming the Traditional Curriculum.

A special feature including essays by Florence Howe and Peggy McIntosh on the impact of the new scholarship on women; reports on programs at Wheaton College, the University of Arizona and Montana State University; and excerpts of the Dinnerstein et al. report (#30) on how to integrate women's studies into the traditional curriculum.

9

Project Evaluation

This section includes references to assessment methods and instruments for use both in program development and assessment and in seminars with faculty to make them aware of the nature and extent of bias in the curriculum. Materials selected for inclusion are those that I have found the most useful in my own work at Montana State University and at other campuses where I have consulted. The first subsection includes some general sources to introduce program leaders to issues and concepts in women's studies evaluation.

GENERAL SOURCES

71. Beere, Carole A. *Women and Women's Issues: A Handbook of Tests and Measures.* San Francisco: Jossey-Bass, 1979.

A listing of 235 measurement instruments used in research regarding women compiled from a search of the literature through 1977. Categories include sex roles, sex stereotypes, sex role prescriptions, gender knowledge, attitudes toward women's issues, and sexual issues. Information for each instrument includes title, author, year it first appeared in the literature, characteristics of respondents, administration and scoring, sample items, reliability and validity, sources and references.

72. Brush, Lorelei R., Alice Ross Gold, and Marni Goldstein White. "The Paradox of Intention and Effect: A Women's Studies Course." *Signs* 3, 4 (Summer 1978): 870–83.

An article that describes the procedures, problems, and results of a study of students enrolled in a one-semester women's studies course. Evaluation design, intended for replication at other institutions, measured the effect of the course on students' self-concept, sex role stereotyping, and commitment to feminist ideology.

73. Howe, Florence. *Seven Years Later: Women's Studies Programs in 1976.* Washington, D.C.: National Advisory Council on Women's Educational Programs, U.S. Department of Health, Education and Welfare, 1977.

A comprehensive study of fifteen women's studies programs across the United States commissioned by the National Advisory

Council on Women's Educational Programs. Indicators of the state of women's studies programs include enrollment growth, variety and depth of course offerings, and impact on the institution. Offers recommendations for further study, development of materials, communication, and programmatic support.

74. Millsap, Mary Ann, Naida Tushnet Bagenstos, and Margaret Talburtt. *Women's Studies Evaluation Handbook*. National Institute of Education Women's Studies Monograph Series. Washington, D.C.: U.S. Government Printing Office, 1979.

A handbook providing information on choosing among types of evaluation, turning program goals into objectives, selecting appropriate research designs, deciding on instruments, analyzing data, and reporting results. Includes abstracts of recent studies and resource materials.

75. Parks, Beverly et al. *Sourcebook of Measures of Women's Educational Equity*. American Institutes for Research. Newton, Mass.: Women's Educational Equity Act (WEEA) Publishing Center, 1982.

A sourcebook of 198 questionnaires, rating scales, inventories, interviews, and checklists to examine procedures, progress, and outcomes of educational equity programs. Content areas include attitudes toward mathematics, sex role perceptions, awareness of racism and sexism, institutional sexism, and materials assessment guidelines. Information for each instrument includes date developed, type, measurement variables, target population, format, administration and scoring, description, sample items, availability, and references.

76. Porter, Nancy M., and Margaret T. Eileenchild [a.k.a. O'Hara]. *The Effectiveness of Women's Studies Teaching*. National Institute of Education Women's Studies Monograph Series. Washington, D.C.: U.S. Government Printing Office, 1980.

A review of literature on the evaluation of teaching effectiveness in women's studies in the "context of several integrative studies in research on teaching and research in the evaluation of teaching." Recommends further research, particularly in the area of cognitive learning.

CLASSROOM INTERACTION

77. Hall, Roberta M., with Bernice R. Sandler. "The Classroom Climate: A Chilly One for Women?" Washington, D.C.: Project on the Status and Education of Women, Association of American Colleges, 1982.

A research report describing and documenting the differences in treatment of female and male university students. Includes recommendations for academic administrators and chief executive officers, student affairs personnel, faculty development programs, faculty, students, and professional associations. Also includes research notes, sample assessment questionnaires, and a selected, annotated list of resources.

78. Jenkins, Mercilee M., Judith M. Gappa, and Janice Pearce. *Removing Bias: Guidelines for Student-Faculty Communication.* Annandale, Va.: Speech Communication Association, 1983.

A set of guidelines for student-faculty communication developed as part of the series "Sex and Gender in the Social Sciences: Reassessing the Introductory Course" by Judith M. Gappa and Janice Pearce (see ##96, 115, 119), "designed to help faculty assess how they are presenting subject matter to students." Consists of two parts: "Student-Faculty Communications," which identifies and provides solutions to problems of stereotyping, bias in language, and patterns of discrimination in classroom interaction; and the "Student Perception Questionnaire," designed to seek student opinions of classroom interaction. Available from Educational Services, Speech Communication Association, 5101 Backlick Road, Suite E, Annandale, VA 22003.

79. Sadker, Myra, and David Sadker. "Between Teacher and Student: Overcoming Sex Bias in Classroom Interaction." In *Sex Equity Handbook for Schools*. New York: Longman, 1982, pp. 96–132.

A curricular unit designed for use in pre-service teacher education programs to help future teachers become knowledgeable about issues of sexism and skilled in approaches to alleviate the problem in schools. Includes instruments for analyzing classroom behaviors for sex-biased teaching patterns and recommendations for developing non-sexist teaching behaviors.

EDUCATIONAL MATERIALS

80. American Psychological Association. Task Force on Issues of Sexual Bias in Graduate Education. "Guidelines for Nonsexist Use of Language." *American Psychologist* 30 (June 1975): 682–84.

A brief article presenting both stylistic and substantive guidelines for avoiding sexism in language use, content, and methodology; based on a content analysis of thirteen textbooks used in graduate education in psychology.

81. American Sociological Association. Committee on the Status of

Women in Sociology. "Sexist Biases in Sociological Research: Problems and Issues." Washington, D.C.: Project on the Status and Education of Women, Association of American Colleges, 1980.

A research report that identifies five aspects of the research process where bias frequently occurs: research problem selection and formulation; review of previous research; selection of population and sample; validity issues; and interpretation of research results. Reprinted from American Sociological Association *Footnotes*, January 1980.

82. Cotera, Martha P., comp. *Checklists for Counteracting Race and Sex Bias in Educational Materials.* Newton, Mass.: WEEA Publishing Center, 1982.

A handbook that provides selected guidelines and checklists to evaluate curriculum materials for use in bilingual/multicultural education programs for race and sex bias. Includes a selected bibliography of guidelines for positive female and male models in textbooks and instruments for materials selection.

83. Froines, Ann. "Integrating Women into the Liberal Arts Curriculum: Some Results of 'A Modest Survey.'" *Women's Studies Newsletter* 8, 4 (Fall/Winter 1980): 11–12.

Report of a faculty survey and student questionnaire administered by a college-wide Committee on the Status of Women at the University of Massachusetts/Boston to assess the impact of the new scholarship on women in the liberal arts curriculum. Discusses the strategy for disseminating the survey, reports the problems encountered, and describes patterns that do not support the goals of integrating women's studies into the curriculum.

84. Gray, Vicky A. "The Image of Women in Psychology Textbooks." *Canadian Psychological Review: Psychologie Canadienne* 18 (1977): 46–55.

An analysis of ten psychology textbooks revealing a bias in psychology toward "the study of male behaviour by male psychologists."

85. Macmillan Publishing Company. *Guidelines for Creating Positive Sexual and Racial Images in Educational Materials.* New York: Macmillan, 1975.

A set of guidelines to overcome sexual and racial bias in educational materials; presents general content guidelines, language use guidelines, and guidelines for textbook art. Presents common stereotypes and gives suggestions for avoiding them. Although developed for children's books, the categories of analysis are adaptable for higher education materials.

86. Sadker, Myra, and David Sadker. *Beyond Pictures and Pronouns: Sexism in Teacher Education Textbooks.* Newton, Mass.: WEEA Publishing Center, 1979.

An analysis of the treatment of women in teacher education textbooks that shows that these texts are more likely to reinforce sexist attitudes and behaviors rather than to reduce them. Provides an understanding of the process of textbook analysis and includes guidelines for teacher education textbooks, suggestions for classroom activities, and supplementary materials.

87. Sadker, Myra, and David Sadker. "Sexism in Teacher Education Texts." *Harvard Educational Review* 50, 1 (February 1980): 36–46.

An analysis of twenty-four teacher education texts that reveal sex bias by omission and imbalance. Offers recommendations for the development of textbooks that will integrate concepts of sex equity into the mainstream of teacher education programs.

CAMPUS ENVIRONMENT

88. Bogart, Karen, Judith Flagle, and Steven Jung. *Institutional Self-Study Guide on Sex Equity for Postsecondary Educational Institutions.* Washington, D.C.: American Institutes for Research, n.d.

Guidelines developed for use by chief executive officers, regional accrediting agencies, and women's advocates for the evaluation of institutional policies, practices, and procedures; based on an empirical study of perceptions of discrimination by 200 key observers. Includes checklists for evaluating conditions affecting students, faculty, administrators, and staff, as well as for the socioeducational climate. Distributed by the Project on the Status and Education of Women.

89. Cloud, Sherrill. *Equity Self-Assessment in Postsecondary Education Institutions.* Boulder, Colo.: National Center for Higher Education Management Systems (NCHEMS), 1980.

A handbook that examines equity considerations for students, faculty, and staff and provides a framework for analysis of equity issues by postsecondary administrators. Available from NCHEMS, Publications Manager, P.O. Drawer P, Boulder, CO 80302.

90. Council of Chief State School Officers. Resource Center on Sex Equity. *Policies for the Future: State Policies, Regulations, and Resources Related to the Achievement of Educational Equity for Females and Males.* Washington, D.C.: Council of Chief State School Officers, 1982.

A resource guide listing—by state—the laws, executive orders, policies, regulations, and resources for educational equity. Available from CCSSO, 379 Hall of the States, 400 North Capitol Street, NW, Washington, DC 20001.

91. Howe, Florence, Suzanne Howard, and Mary Jo Boehm Strauss, eds. *Everywoman's Guide to Colleges and Universities*. Old Westbury, N.Y.: The Feminist Press, 1982.

A guide that provides an overview of issues affecting women as students and a description of how to assess the "health" of an institution for its women students. Includes ratings for 600 colleges and universities in three areas: women in leadership, women and the curriculum, and women and athletics. Information for the ratings was compiled by questionnaire (copy included in the Appendix of that book) and from data of the National Council on Education Statistics.

10

Course Revision Models

This section includes published essays and syllabi for courses developed to integrate the study of women into the curriculum. It does not include collections of syllabi for women's studies courses, except for those recent collections that integrate the experience of women of differing race, ethnicity, class, and sexual identity into the women's studies curriculum. Project leaders are referred to the review essays in *Signs* (#138) for additional references to discipline-specific material.

GENERAL COLLECTIONS

92. Handsher, Sandra. *Integrating Women-Related Materials into [the] Traditional Curriculum*. Novato, Calif.: Indian Valley Colleges, 1979.

The final product of a college-funded project that encouraged instructors to use women-related materials in their courses. Includes instruments to survey the amount of women-related material in courses and to analyze textbooks for sex bias as well as bibliographies to aid in curriculum development in anthropology, art history, biology, English, health education, management, political science, and vocational education. Out of print. Available through the Indian Valley Colleges Library, Novato, CA 94947.

93. O'Donnell, Sheryl, and Barbara M. Shaver, eds. *Women's Scholarship: A Curriculum Handbook*. Grand Forks, N. Dak.: University of North Dakota, 1983.

A collection of essays on integrating the new scholarship on women into the university curriculum by faculty who participated in the University of North Dakota's Women's Equity Project, 1980–81. Disciplines include anthropology, business, career planning, economics, education, German, history, journalism, mathematics, music, nursing, science, social work, sociology, statistics, and women's studies. Available from Women's Equity Committee, P.O. Box 8161, University Station, Grand Forks, ND 58202.

BLACK WOMEN'S STUDIES

94. Black Studies/Women's Studies Faculty Development Project.

149

Black Studies/Women's Studies: A Long Overdue Partnership. Courses Addressing Issues of Race, Gender and Culture. Mimeographed. N.p., n.d.

Collection of course syllabi developed under a grant from the Fund for the Improvement of Postsecondary Education, and co-directed by Johnnella Butler (Smith College) and Margo Culley (University of Massachusetts-Amherst). Includes syllabi for courses in Afro-American studies, American studies, music, political theory, history, sociology, psychology, philosophy, communications, literature, and women's studies. Out of print. May be available in certain library collections.

95. Conklin, Nancy Faires, Brenda McCallum, and Marcia Wade. *The Culture of Southern Black Women: Approaches and Materials.* University, Ala.: University of Alabama, Archive of American Minority Cultures and the Women's Studies Program, 1983.

A curriculum guide produced by scholars of black studies, women's studies, Southern studies, and folklore between 1980–83 under a grant from the Fund for the Improvement of Postsecondary Education. Contains the following parts: an introduction describing the project, organization, and use of the guide; three thematic sections—Southern Black Female Identity, Women's Roles in Afro-American Culture and Community, and Cultural Expressions of Southern Black Culture—that contain suggestions for both pedagogical approaches and appropriate multidisciplinary materials and resources; a set of guidelines for student field research projects; and an alphabetical list of print, visual, and audio resources assembled by the project. Available from Women's Studies Program, University of Alabama, P.O. Box 1391, University, AL 35486.

COMMUNICATION STUDIES
See Jenkins, Mercilee M. et al., *Removing Bias: Guidelines for Student-Faculty Communication, #78.*

ECONOMICS
96. Gappa, Judith M., and Janice Pearce. *Sex and Gender in the Social Sciences: Reassessing the Introductory Course. Principles of Microeconomics.* Mimeographed. San Francisco: San Francisco State University, 1982.

Extensive guidelines for integrating content on women into an introductory microeconomics course and for assessing student-faculty communication in the classroom. Material arranged by standard textbook topics and chapters, giving practical suggestions on how to incorporate information on sex and gender into class discussion; includes references and notes for supplementary reading. Available from Judith M. Gappa, Associate Provost, San Francisco State University, 1600 Holloway Avenue, N-AD 455, San Francisco, CA 94132.

97. Miller, John A. "Integrating the New Research on Women into Economics: A Report and a Bibliography." In Spanier et al., **#62**, pp. 233–51.

A report of the Wheaton College Economics Department's integration project in which new research on women was integrated through lecture format into introductory courses. Includes a bibliography of materials on women in the modern economy arranged under the categories: studies of women in the economy; women's work inside and outside the home; histories of women's work; selections on feminist theory; and statistical sources. Also includes an annotated bibliography of selections suited to introductory economics.

EDUCATION
See Sadker, Myra, and David Sadker. "Between Teacher and Student: Overcoming Sex Bias in Classroom Interaction,"**#79.**

ENGINEERING
98. LeBold, William K. "Putting It All Together: A Model Program for Women Entering Engineering." Newton, Mass.: WEEA Publishing Center, 1982.

A model career preparation program developed for first-year engineering women at Purdue University. Key elements described are a course designed to provide engineering and career information and practical experience; a means of evaluating the methods and results; wide dissemination of all useful information generated by the experimental course; and the collection of information relevant to programs for women in engineering. Includes an annotated bibliography on women in engineering and women in management.

ENGLISH EDUCATION
99. Folsom, Jack. "Teaching about Sexism and Language in a Traditional Setting: Surmounting the Obstacles." *Women's Studies Quarterly* 11, 1 (Spring 1983): 12–15.

An article providing a model for training future teachers of English in how to teach about sexism and language in the public schools.

EXPERIENTIAL EDUCATION
100. Fisher, Jerilyn, and Elaine Reuben, eds. *The Women's Studies*

Service Learning Handbook: From the Classroom to the Community.
College Park, Md.: National Women's Studies Association, 1981.

A handbook that provides varied approaches to women's studies
service learning and an "overview of the dynamics of field experience
education from a feminist perspective"; developed through the National Women's Studies Association Project to Improve Service Learning in Women's Studies. Includes essays on experiential learning in
relation to women's studies; case studies of institutional adaptations
of women's studies service learning; perspectives of students and
agency supervisors; and sample course descriptions, bibliographies,
learning tools, and other materials for developing service learning
courses.

GEOGRAPHY

101. Rengert, Arlene C., and Janice J. Monk. *Women and Spatial
Change: Learning Resources for Social Science Courses.* Dubuque,
Iowa: Kendall/Hunt, 1982.

A collection of six units designed "for use in a variety of survey-
type introductory courses that rely on textbooks that lack gender balance." Units represent different types of instruction and different
levels of balance and include: Women and Agricultural Landscapes;
Landscapes of the Home; Geographic Perspectives on Social Change:
The Example of Women in Crime; Locational Decision Making: The
Case of the Day Care Center; Village to Barriada: Contemporary Female Migration to Cities in Latin America; and Farm to Factory: Female Industrial Migration in Early 19th Century New England. Each
unit contains a student reading and an instructor packet of key concepts, materials for lecture/discussion, exercises, and bibliography.

102. "Women in Geographic Curricula."*Journal of Geography* 77, 5
(September/October 1978): 164–91.

A special issue coordinated by Bonnie Loyd and Arlene Rengert
that provides an overview of the issues and suggestions for the development of courses that teach women's role in geography. See the
introduction by Loyd and Rengert; "Teaching Women's Role in
Changing the Face of the Earth: How and Why" by Marie Deatherage-
Newsom; "Geography in Women's Studies at Salem College" by
Mildred Berman; and "Feminist Approaches in Teaching Geography"
by David R. Lee.

HISTORY

103. *HER STORY: 1620–1980, A Curriculum Guide for American History Teachers.* Princeton, N.J.: Woodrow Wilson National Fellowship
Foundation, 1981.

A guide to the inclusion of the study of women in American history covering five periods: Colonial to Revolutionary (Carol R. Berkin); the Early Republic (Linda K. Kerber); the Progressive Era, 1870–1920 (Lois W. Banner); and Modern America (Sara Evans). Includes examples from primary sources, suggestions for paper topics, and an eighteen-page bibliography. Available from Woodrow Wilson National Fellowship Foundation, P.O. Box 642, Princeton, NJ 08540.

104. Lerner, Gerda. *Teaching Women's History*. Washington, D.C.: American Historical Association, 1981.

A pamphlet that provides an overview of the field of women's history and its methods and techniques; designed for "those wanting to incorporate women's history into existing survey or topic courses" and "those wanting to teach separate units or courses on the subject." Includes chapters on the historiography of women's history to 1970; on concepts and strategies for teaching women's history; on topics in teaching women's history; and on teaching about the female experience, including black women, Native American women, Hispanic women and Asian American women. Bibliographic notes and sources are provided. Available from AHA, 400 A Street, SE, Washington, DC 20003.

105. Organization of American Historians. *Restoring Women to History: Materials for U.S. I and II*. 2 vols. Bloomington, Ind.: Organization of American Historians, 1983.

A guide for the integration of the study of women into survey courses in United States history. Organized by standard chapters found in major textbooks in American history. Includes lectures, suggested discussion questions and assignments, bibliographies for both students and instructors, and supplementary readings for instructors. Developed under a grant from the Fund for the Improvement of Postsecondary Education. Available from OAH, 112 North Bryan, Bloomington, IN 47401.

106. Fox-Genovese, Elizabeth, and Susan Mosher Stuard. *Restoring Women to History: Materials for Western Civilization I and II*. 2 vols. Bloomington, Ind.: Organization of American Historians, 1983.

A guide for the integration of the study of women into survey of Western civilization courses. Organized chronologically by standard textbook chapters; includes lectures, suggested discussion questions and assignments, bibliographies for both students and instructors, and supplementary readings for instructors. See ordering address in #105.

LITERATURE
107. Berkson, Dorothy, and Stephen Knox. "Reteaching American

literature." Unpublished manuscript. [Portland, Oreg.: Lewis and Clark College, 1983.]

An article focusing on the authors' experiences in teaching two traditional periods of American literature: the mid-nineteenth century and the 1920s and 1950s. Discusses pairings of male and female writers (e.g., Melville, Stowe; Mailer, Walker), and thematic approaches that lend themselves readily to considerations of gender in shaping literature and literary criticism. Illustrates how traditional periodization has excluded considerations of female writers and provides a framework of analysis adaptable to other literature courses. Available from the authors, Department of English, Lewis and Clark College, Portland, OR 97219.

108. Cole, Phyllis, and Deborah Lambert. "Gender and Race in American Literature: An Exploration of the Discipline and a Proposal for Two New Courses." Working Paper No. 115. Wellesley, Mass.: Wellesley College Center for Research on Women, n.d.

A paper that provides a brief overview of "the special masculinity of the new-world myth" as perpetuated by scholars of American literature in the nineteenth and twentieth centuries; reviews the feminist critical response to racism and sexism in the traditional canon; and offers a theoretical and historical argument for reconstructing American literature as envisaged by the Reconstructing American Literature Project (see #109). Two course models are provided. One, by Lambert, New Hampshire Women Writers: Recovering Lost Literature, illustrates in an experiential learning mode for students how a literary canon is formed. Cole's course, American Romanticisms, 1815–1870, considers thematic units in chronological sequence, such as literary nationalism and literary domesticity, first-person voices and inner worlds, and "self-reliance" as an American ideology.

109. Lauter, Paul, ed. *Reconstructing American Literature: Courses, Syllabi, Issues*. Old Westbury, N.Y.: The Feminist Press, 1983.

A collection of sixty-seven syllabi "that differ significantly from those of most [American literature] courses in content and often in organization"; includes, for most syllabi, introductory statements on course methodology by the instructors, bibliographies or reading lists, and student assignments. Also includes a general introduction by Lauter to the practical and theoretical issues involved in reconstructing American literature and a model chronology by Jean Fagan Yellin. Syllabi are divided into four categories: introductory courses, advanced period courses, genre courses, and thematic courses.

MEDICINE

110. American Medical Women's Association. *Women in Medical Academia*. Newton, Mass.: WEEA Publishing Center, 1982.

Two workbooks presenting fifteen courses and a 3½ day workshop. Surveys the male doctor/female patient relationship, the role of textbooks in medical training, and the history of women in medicine. Includes a listing of support networks for women in medicine.

MUSIC
111. Hayes, Deborah. "Syllabus for Music 475: Women Composers." Unpublished manuscript. Boulder, Colo.: University of Colorado, [1982].

Syllabus and supporting materials for a women's studies course on Women Composers; material suitable for integration into general music history courses. Contains the course introduction; short biographies and bibliographies of women composers; a list of recordings; and sample examinations. Available from the author, Department of Music History and Literature, University of Colorado, Boulder, CO 80309.

POLITICAL SCIENCE
112. American Political Science Association. *Citizenship and Change: Women and American Politics*. 9 vols. Washington, D.C.: American Political Science Association, 1983–84.

A field-tested series of units developed by the APSA Task Force on Women and American Government under the project "Citizenship and Change: Women and American Politics"; designed to supplement or replace introductory courses in American government and politics. Units include: *How Feminist Theory Reconstructs American Government and Politics* by Diane L. Fowlkes (1983); *Women's Movements: Organizing for Change in the 1980s* by Joyce Gelb and Ethel Klein (1983); *Women and American Political Organizations and Institutions* by Milda K. Hedblom (1983); *Women, Political Action, and Political Participation* by Virginia Sapiro (1983); *Feminism and the Growth of the American Polity* by Mary L. Shanley and Shelby Lewis (1983); *Men, Women and State Violence: Government and the Military* by Judith H. Stiehm with Michelle Saint-Germain (1983); *Women in the Judicial Process* by Beverly B. Cook, Karen O'Connor, and Susette M. Talarico; *Family and Public Policy* by Irene Diamond (forthcoming); *Images and Films: Race and Gender* by Dianne Pinderhughes (forthcoming); *Constitutional Principles* by Sarah Slavin (forthcoming). Available from Educational Affairs, APSA, 1527 New Hampshire Avenue, NW, Washington, DC 20036.

113. Pratt, Ray. "Reflections on Teaching about Women in Two Courses in Political Thought." *Women's Studies Quarterly* 11, 1 (Spring 1983): 15–19.

A discussion of the omission of women in political theory and two course models for classical political theory and modern political thought. Includes a short annotated bibliography.

PSYCHOLOGY

114. American Psychological Association. Women's Programs Office. "Resources for Teaching the History of Women in Psychology." Mimeographed. Washington, D.C.: American Psychological Association, 1981.

A beginning bibliography of resources and literature available, including publications specific to psychology, bibliographies, general publications, resources, archives, and media. Available from Women's Programs Office, APA, 1200 17 Street, NW, Washington, DC 20036.

115. Gappa, Judith M., and Janice Pearce. *Sex and Gender in the Social Sciences: Reassessing the Introductory Course. Introductory Psychology.* Washington, D.C.: American Psychological Association, 1982.

Extensive guidelines for integrating content on women into introductory psychology courses. Arranged by standard textbook topics; gives practical suggestions on how to incorporate information on sex and gender into classroom discussions; also includes references for supplementary readings. See ordering address in #114.

116. Rands, Marylyn. *Psychology By, About, and For Women: Revising the Introductory Curriculum.* In Spanier et al., #62, pp. 302–308.

A report of the Wheaton College Psychology Department's integration project; summarizes project planning and curriculum design; describes experiences of the teachers; and presents a summary of student evaluations

SOCIAL WORK

117. Brandwein, Ruth A., and Anne E. Wheelock. "A New Course Model for Content on Women's Issues in Social Work Education." *Journal of Education for Social Work* 14, 3 (Fall 1978): 20–26.

Article that describes the development and content of a student-designed, graduate-level course on women and social work; discusses four educational issues in course design: separation vs. integration of course content; sexism vs. racism; intellectual vs. experiential learning; and women only vs. coeducational enrollment.

118. Rosenman, Linda, and Roy Ruckdeschel. "Catch 1234B: Integrating Material on Women into the Social Work Research Curriculum." *Journal of Education for Social Work* 17, 2 (Spring 1981): 5–11.

An article that examines how sex bias has affected the conduct and teaching of research in social work curricula; explores assumptions underlying research models and implications for the development of research-based knowledge about women. Also describes special efforts to revise the curriculum in response to the 1977 Council on Social Work Education's mandate (Standard 1234B) to incorporate material on women.

SOCIOLOGY
119. Gappa, Judith M., and Janice Pearce. *Sex and Gender in the Social Sciences: Reassessing the Introductory Course. Introductory Sociology.* Washington, D.C.: American Sociological Association, 1983.

Extensive guidelines for integrating content on women into introductory sociology courses and for assessing student-faculty communication in the classroom. Arranged by standard textbook chapters and topics; gives practical suggestions for incorporating material on sex and gender into class discussion; also includes references to supplementary materials by topic. Available from Teaching Resources Center, ASA, 1722 N Street, NW, Washington, DC 20036.

WOMEN'S STUDIES
120. Elwell, Ellen Sue Levi, and Edward R. Levenson, eds. and comps. *The Jewish Women's Studies Guide.* New York: Biblio Press, 1982.

A collection of fifteen syllabi and reading lists from college courses focusing on Jewish women, general courses integrating the study of Jewish women, and adult and continuing education classes.

121. Goddard-Cambridge Graduate Program in Social Change. *Breaking the Silence: Seven Courses in Women's Studies.* Newton, Mass.: WEEA Publishing Center, 1979.

A collection of seven interdisciplinary courses for adolescent and adult women that "seeks to address the effects of sex role stereotyping on the lives of Third World, poor, working-class, and institutionalized women." Includes a user's guide; a section on general resources; and course goals, descriptions, and reading lists for Black Women Writers, Introduction to Women's History in the United States, Reading and Writing about Women's Lives, Sex Roles and Socialization, Women in Cross-Cultural Perspective, Women in Prison, and Women and Their Working Lives.

See also Cruikshank, *Lesbian Studies*, **#5.**

11

Periodicals

This section contains periodicals that I highly recommend for keeping abreast of feminist scholarship and publishing. Readers are referred especially to *Feminist Collections* (#124), *Feminist Periodicals* (#125), and *New Books on Women and Feminism* (#130), all available from the Office of the Women's Studies Librarian-at-Large, University of Wisconsin System. I have chosen for the most part to include general rather than discipline-specific or literary journals and those focusing on feminism in higher education, although representative periodicals focusing on broader feminist issues and on writings by women of color have been included. Founding date and publishing frequency are given in parentheses after the name of the periodical; the editor's name and subscription address are also included.

122. *Conditions* (1976; semiannual)

A "feminist magazine of writing by women, with an emphasis on writing by lesbians" that "includes work in a variety of styles by both published and unpublished writers of many different backgrounds." Contains poetry, short fiction, excerpts from novels, drama, reviews, and articles. Editorial collective. *Conditions*, P.O. Box 56A, Van Brunt Station, Brooklyn, NY 11215.

123. *Connexions: An International Women's Quarterly* (1981; quarterly)

A journal of translations from the international feminist press "conceived as a means of fostering an international feminist network." Each issue focuses on a specific theme and carries direct translations of articles and interviews from feminist sources in other countries. Editorial collective. *Connexions*, 4228 Telegraph Avenue, Oakland, CA 94609.

124. *Feminist Collections: Women's Studies Library Resources in Wisconsin* (1980; quarterly)

A periodical issued by the Office of the Women's Studies Librarian-at-Large, University of Wisconsin System, focusing on feminist librarianship, publishing, and archival and research sources. Includes feature articles, editorials, news, book reviews, bibliographies, notes on periodicals, and review essays on a particular topic. Susan Searing and Catherine Loeb, Editors. 112A Memorial Library, 728 State Street, Madison, WI 53706.

125. *Feminist Periodicals: A Current Listing of Contents* (1981; quarterly)
A periodical issued by the Women's Studies Librarian-at-Large, University of Wisconsin System, that provides essential information for all English-language feminist publications with national or regional readership, with an emphasis on scholarly journals and small press offerings. Reproduces table-of-contents pages of major feminist periodicals. Susan Searing, Editor. 112A Memorial Library, 728 State Street, Madison, WI 53706.

126. *FS, Feminist Studies* (1972; 3/year)
Founded "to encourage analytic responses to feminist issues and to open new areas of research, criticism and speculation." Contains historical and critical articles, reviews, poetry, artwork, and reports from the women's movement. Claire G. Moses, Managing Editor. Women's Studies Program, University of Maryland, College Park, MD 20742.

127. *Frontiers: A Journal of Women's Studies* (1975; 3/year)
Published to bridge the "gap between university and community women; [and] to find a balance between academic and popular views on issues common to women." Features articles on a special theme, book reviews, poetry, and short fiction. Kathi George, Editor. Women's Studies Program, University of Colorado, Boulder, CO 80309.

128. *International Journal of Women's Studies* (1978; 5/year)
A Canadian interdisciplinary journal that publishes historical and critical articles and book reviews. Sherri Clarkson, Editor. Eden Press, P.O. Box 51, St. Albans, VT 05478.

129. *Journal of Educational Equity and Leadership* (1980; quarterly)
Journal "directed at the enhancement of equity for women American Indians, Asian-Americans, Blacks, Hispanics, and other populations to provide leaders with ideas for advancing educational equity, to stimulate research, to facilitate communication, and to provide a forum for emergent practices on equity." L. Dean Webb, Editor. Arizona State University, Department of Educational Administration, 107 Farmer Building, Tempe, AZ 85287.

130. *New Books on Women and Feminism* (1979; 3/year)
A selected list of books, periodicals, and non-print materials culled

primarily from reviews and publishers' catalogs; includes both commercial and small press publications. Annotated entries, arranged by subject, include "all bibliographic information readily available." Issued by the Office of the Women's Studies Librarian-at-Large. Susan Searing, Editor. 112A Memorial Library, 728 State Street, Madison, WI 53706.

131. *off our backs* (1970; 11/year)
A radical feminist publication that contains national and international news and regular coverage of topics of work, health, prison, violence, education, legal, and lesbian issues, with particular emphasis on women outside the "mainstream" of society. Also contains interviews, book reviews, and coverage of feminist conferences and meetings. Editorial collective. *off our backs*, 1841 Columbia Road, NW, Room 212, Washington, DC 20009.

132. *Plainswoman* (1977; monthly excluding February and August)
Regional journal seeks to provide "a regional perspective and interpretation of issues that have national (and international) significance." Publishes articles, essays, fiction, poetry, and reviews for and about women in the Plains region, with a special emphasis on rural women. Elizabeth Hampsten, Editor. P.O. Box 8027, Grand Forks, ND 58202.

133. *Psychology of Women Quarterly* (1976; quarterly)
Journal sponsored by Division 35 of the American Psychological Association. Includes empirical studies, critical reviews, theoretical articles, and invited book reviews which address issues concerning behavioral studies, role development and change, career choice and training, education, discrimination, therapeutic processes, and sexuality. Nancy Henley, Editor. Human Sciences Press, 72 Fifth Avenue, New York, NY 10011.

134. *Quest: A Feminist Quarterly* (1974; quarterly)
A journal that focuses on "long-term, in-depth feminist political analysis and ideological development." Joan Twiggs, Editor. P.O. Box 8843, Washington, DC 20003.

135. *Resources for Feminist Research/Documentation sur la Recherche Féministe* (1972; quarterly)
Formerly the Canadian Newsletter of Research on Women. Provides information on women's studies teaching and research in England, Europe, and Canada, with some United States sources. Includes book reviews, review essays, bibliographies, innovative syllabi, and archival holdings in women's history. Editorial collective.

Centre for Women's Studies Education, Ontario Institute for Studies in Education, 252 Bloor Street West, Toronto, Ontario, M5S 1V6, Canada.

136. *Sage: A Scholarly Journal on Black Women* (1984; 2/year)
A journal whose purpose is "(1) to provide an interdisciplinary forum for critical issues relating to Black women, (2) to promote feminist scholarship, and (3) to disseminate new knowledge about Black women to a broad audience." Issues are organized around a theme and include a readers' forum, articles, interviews, resource and research updates, documents, reviews, and news items. Patricia Bell Scott and Beverly Guy-Sheftall, Editors. *Sage*, P.O. Box 42741, Atlanta, GA 30311.

137. *Sex Roles: A Journal of Research* (1975; monthly)
Journal that contains articles on empirical research relating to sex roles, and book reviews. Phyllis A. Katz, Editor. Plenum Publishing Corporation, 233 Spring Street, New York, NY 10013.

138. *Signs: Journal of Women in Culture and Society* (1975; quarterly)
Journal featuring theoretical and research articles, essays, and reviews related to the new scholarship on women, letter/comments, and archival notes. Jean O'Barr, Editor. The University of Chicago Press, Journals Division, P.O. Box 37005, Chicago, IL 60637.

139. *Studies on Women Abstracts* (1983; quarterly)
An international abstracting service focusing on education, employment, women in the family and the community, medicine and health, female sex and gender role socialization, social policy, the social psychology of women, female culture, media treatment of women, and historical studies. Entries are grouped in two sections: journal articles, arranged alphabetically by journal title; and books, arranged alphabetically by author. Cumulative author and subject indexes are included in the final issue of each volume. Rosemary Deem, Editor. Carfax Publishing Company, Hopkinton Office and Research Park, 35 South Street, Hopkinton, MA 01748.

140. *Third Woman* (1981; 2/year)
Journal of creative and critical work by, about, and on behalf of U.S. Latinas and Third World women in general. Norma Alarcon, Editor. Chicano-Riqueno Studies, Ballantine Hall 849, Indiana University, Bloomington, IN 47405.

141. *WLW Journal* (1976; quarterly)
Journal published by the Women Library Workers. Contains

articles on feminism in library science; news of general interest to women's programs; critical reviews of books, films, records, periodicals, pamphlets, and other media by and for women. Carol Starr, Editor. WLW, 2027 Parker Street, Berkeley, CA 94704.

142. *Women's Review of Books: An Independent Journal* (1983; monthly)

A review of feminist writing in all fields; autobiography, fiction, and poetry by women. Occasional review essays on trends in a particular area of women's studies, on an individual's work, or on the feminist writing within a particular ethnic or religious group. Linda Gardiner, Editor. Dept. FP, The Women's Review of Books, 18 Norfolk Terrace, Wellesley, MA 02181.

143. *Women's Studies* (1972; 3/year)

A forum for the presentation of scholarship and criticism about women in the fields of literature, history, art, sociology, law, political science, economics, anthropology, and the sciences. Also contains book reviews, poetry, and short fiction. Wendy Martin, Editor. Gordon and Breach Science, Ltd., Publishers, 42 William IV Street, London WC2, England.

144. *Women's Studies International Forum* (1978; bimonthly)

Formerly Women's Studies International Quarterly. Publishes research communications, review articles, book reviews, and symposia reports that reflect the multidisciplinary and international nature of women's studies both inside and outside formal education. Dale Spender, Editor. Pergamon Press, Maxwell House, Fairview Park, Elmsford, NY 10523.

145. *Women's Studies Quarterly* (1972; quarterly)

Formerly Women's Studies Newsletter. Contains articles relating to the theory and practice of women's studies and current efforts to transforms the curriculum, editorials, letters, features, reviews, resources. Provides an annual listing of Women's Studies Programs, Centers for Research on Women, and Projects to Transform the Curriculum. Alternate issues focus on themes, for example, "Teaching about Mothering." Includes Women's Studies International. Nancy Porter, Editor. The Feminist Press, Box 334, Old Westbury, NY 11568.

12

Bibliographies

146. "American Women of Color: A Bibliography of Current Sources." Mimeographed. Madison, Wis.: Women's Studies Librarian-at-Large, University of Wisconsin System, 1979.

A bibliography of articles, books, and government documents, primarily in the social sciences, from 1977–79, on Asian-American women, black women, Chicanas, Latinas, Native American women, and women of color. Arranged by ethnic group, with an index of specific subject titles.

147. Ballou, Patricia K. "Bibliographies for Research on Women." *Signs* 3, 2 (Winter 1977): 436–50.

A review of "significant bibliographic works" that appeared between 1970 and 1977; arranged by topical areas: general bibliographies, history, literature, anthropology and area studies, economics and employment, education, politics and law, sociology, psychology, and health. Additional titles appear at the end for these areas, and for the arts, philosophy, religious studies, and the professions.

148. Ballou, Patricia K. *Women: A Bibliography of Bibliographies.* Boston: G.K. Hall, 1980.

A 557-item annotated bibliography of bibliographies "concerned primarily with women or with a topic traditionally associated with women." Includes works published between 1970 and 1979; excludes reprints of earlier works, lists of nonsexist children's books, material dealing with one or several individuals, nonprint media, and newsletters of women's caucuses. Criteria for selection included scope, availability, organization, and commentary. Arranged by general and interdisciplinary works (e.g., history, literature), publications of one type or format (e.g., special periodical issues, dissertations), geographical subjects, and topical subjects.

149. Bataille, Gretchen. "Bibliography on Native American Women." *Concerns* 10 (Summer 1980): 16–27.

An annotated bibliography providing listings of biographies, autobiographies, anthropological and ethnographical studies, and literature by and about Native American women. Also includes a listing of journals that frequently publish articles about Native American women.

150. Borenstein, Audrey. *Older Women in 20th-Century America: A Selected Annotated Bibliography.* New York: Garland, 1982.

An 885-item, cross-disciplinary, annotated bibliography of books, articles, government publications, conference proceedings, and position papers on women over the age of forty. Arranged by topical areas including references to social science literature, fiction, biography, autobiography, oral histories, and personal documents by older women. Indexed by author.

151. Cardinale, Susan, comp. *Anthologies By and About Women: An Analytical Index.* Westport, Conn.: Greenwood Press, 1982.

An index designed "to serve as a guide to essays, stories, drama, and the like, which are not analyzed during the process of book cataloging, indexed in major reference tools, or listed as separate items in bibliographies"; includes titles published after 1960, with some older volumes reissued during the 1960s and 1970s. Indexed by subject, key word, contributors, and editors; also reproduces the contents of each collection.

152. Castelli, Elizabeth, comp. *Selected Bibliography.* Mimeographed. Claremont, Calif.: Claremont Colleges, 1983.

A bibliography compiled for the Claremont Colleges Conference, "Traditions and Transitions: Women's Studies and the Balanced Curriculum"; designed to introduce faculty to feminist scholarship in the disciplines. References are grouped under the headings of theories of women's studies, general bibliographies, women's studies periodicals, anthropology, arts, economics, history, literature, math and science, philosophy and religion, political science, sociology, and Third World women. Reprinted in Spanier et al., #62.

153. Chapman, Anne. *Feminist Resources for Schools and Colleges: A Guide to Curricular Materials.* 3rd Rev. ed. Old Westbury, N.Y.: The Feminist Press (forthcoming).

A comprehensive annotated bibliography of nonsexist books, pamphlets, audio-visual aids, and other materials for teachers and students, pre-school through college. Subject areas covered include American and European history, literature, the social sciences, mathematics, and art.

154. Cotera, Martha P., comp., and Nella Cunningham, ed. *Multicultural Women's Sourcebook: Materials Guide for Use in*

Women's Studies and Bilingual Multicultural Programs. Newton, Mass.: WEEA Publishing Center, 1982.

A sourcebook of 2,000 entries for materials about Asian, Asian-American, African, Afro-American, Cuban, Mexican-American, Puerto Rican, Middle Eastern, Jewish, Native American, and white ethnic American women. Includes a directory of publishers.

155. Eichler, Margrit, John Marecki, and Jennifer Newton. *Women: A Bibliography of Special Periodical Issues (1960–1975).* Special Publication No. 3. Toronto: Canadian Newsletter of Research on Women, 1976.

A special publication of the *Canadian Newsletter of Research on Women* that identifies special issues on women for the years 1960–75; provides bibliographic information and contents for the areas of anthropology, arts and literature, black studies, business administration, criminology, education, folklore, futurology, health, history, industrial and labor relations, social science, philosophy, political economy, political science, psychology, primatology, religion, sexology, social psychology, sociology, and work. Special issues were defined as those not normally devoted to women; selection was based primarily on academic quality. See ordering address in #135.

156. Green, Rayna. *Native American Women: A Contextual Bibliography.* Bloomington: Indiana University Press, 1983.

An expanded library edition of an offprint version originally published in 1981 by the OHOYO Resource Center (#206). Contains 677 annotated references to works by and about American, Alaskan, and Canadian Native women published between 1620 and 1980. Works are listed alphabetically by author and indexed by subject and date. An introductory essay provides a chronological review of the material and a " 'progress' report on the trends and issues that characterize literature on and by Native North American women."

157. Haber, Barbara. *Women in America: A Guide to Books, 1963–1975.* Champaign, Ill.: University of Illinois Press, 1981.

An updated edition of a bibliography of books on American women since 1963 originally published in 1978 by G.K. Hall and developed for "college teachers not familiar with recent literature on women's issues who would like to incorporate such materials into introductory courses . . ." Includes books that focus on the impact of the women's movement on both academic research and popular writing. Arranged by subject area, including black women and Native American women; education; history; law and politics; literature, fine arts and popular culture; psychology; religion; sex roles; sexuality; and work. The new material on books published between 1976 and 1979 is in the form of a review essay arranged by the same subject areas, with the addition of a section on lesbian feminism.

158. Hall, Paula Quick, Mary Jane Tehin, and Rachel Warner. "Bibliography on Women in Science, Engineering and Mathematics." Mimeographed. Washington, D.C.: American Association for the Advancement of Science, [1980].

A bibliography that "focuses on the United States, omits research on the medical or health professions, and excludes publications before 1966"; arranged alphabetically by author and compiled chiefly through computer searches by ERIC (Educational Resources Information Center), SSIE (Smithsonian Science Information Exchange), and NTIS (National Technical Information Service). Reprinted from Michele L. Aldrich and Paula Quick Hall, *Programs in Science, Mathematics and Engineering for Women in the United States: 1966–1978* (Washington, D.C.: American Association for the Advancement of Science, 1980). Available from AAAS, 1776 Massachusetts Avenue, NW, Washington, DC 20036.

159. Hinding, Andrea, ed. *Women's History Sources: A Guide to Archives and Manuscript Collections in the United States.* New York: R. R. Bowker, 1979.

A two-volume set providing descriptions of more than 18,000 archival collections in the United States containing primary source information relevant to women. Entries are described by title, type of document, inclusive dates and collection size, and access information. Includes comment on the correspondence and diaries of unknown women; journals of the sisters, mothers, and wives of famous men; the working drafts of contemporary women writers; and the writings of famous women in American history.

160. Kumagai, Gloria. *America's Women of Color: Integrating Cultural Diversity into Non-Sex-Biased Curricula. Minority Women: An Annotated Bibliography.* Newton, Mass.: WEEA Publishing Center, 1982.

A bibliography designed to supplement a teacher-training program on Integrating Cultural Diversity into Non-Sex-Biased Curriculum, produced with support from a grant from the Women's Educational Equity Act Program. Organized by minority group under sections on elementary resources, secondary resources, postsecondary and teacher resources, elementary audiovisual resources, and secondary audiovisual resources. Selection criteria included authorship by minority women, knowledge of subject, readability, interest level, and availability.

161. Loeb, Catherine, comp. *Black Women's Studies and Black Feminist Politics: Selected Sources 1970–1983.* Mimeographed. Madison, Wis.: Women's Studies Librarian-at-Large, University of Wisconsin System, 1983.

A listing of black studies/women's studies/black women's studies, including comparative perspectives, a history of black women, literature, anthologies and criticism, social science, special issues of periodicals, and bibliographies related to black women.

162. Loeb, Catherine. "La Chicana: A Bibliographic Survey." *Frontiers* 5, 2 (Summer 1980): 59–74.

A bibliographic review essay that provides an introduction to English-language materials on Chicanas, with an emphasis on recent, easily accessible works. Describes and evaluates background sources in Chicana studies as well as sources in history, literature, education, employment, law, medicine, health, sexuality, reproduction, welfare, the family, and politics. Also includes a review of periodicals that regularly publish articles or have dedicated special issues to literature on and by Chicanas, and a 300-item bibliography.

163. Mehlman, T., ed. *Annotated Guide to Women's Periodicals in the U.S. and Canada* 2, 2 (October 1983).

A selected list of periodicals that present "positive images of women" and are "primarily managed and written by women." Periodicals are grouped by subject (e.g., Academic, Asian Women, Lesbian, Older Women, etc.) and occasionally geographically within subject. Information provided for each periodical includes name, address, frequency of publication, subscription prices, writer's guidelines, and a brief description of its character. Indexed alphabetically and by state. Available from the Women's Programs Office, Earlham College, Richmond, IN 47373.

164. Moore, Kathryn M., and Peter A. Wollitzer. *Women in Higher Education: A Contemporary Bibliography.* Washington, D.C.: The National Association of Women Deans, Counselors and Administrators, 1979.

An annotated bibliography of research on women in higher education between 1970 and 1978 arranged according to the roles women hold as undergraduates, graduate students, faculty, and administrators; also includes a section on historical and contemporary perspectives and on bibliographies and demographic studies. Available from NAWDAC, Suite 210, 1325 18th Street, NW, Washington, DC 20036.

165. Nelson, Margaret F., and M. Frances Walton, comps. *OHOYO IKHANA: A Bibliography of American Indian—Alaska Native Curriculum Materials.* Wichita Falls, Kans.: OHOYO Resource Center, 1982.

A 1,200-item bibliography of curriculum materials and periodical articles developed primarily within Indian cultures and designed to assist the classroom teacher "to teach Indian history as American history and not as a separate unit"; suitable for primary grades through postsecondary. Arranged by source and indexed by region, audio-visual materials, bibliographies, and resource personnel.

166. Newton, Jennifer L., and Carol Zavitz, comps. *Women: A Bibliography of Special Periodical Issues.* Toronto: Canadian Newsletter of Research on Women, 1978.

A volume that updates the earlier volume by Eichler et al. (#154) and lists approximately 375 special issues on women; provides information on availability, publishers' addresses, and table of contents. Areas include anthropology, art and architecture, black and minority studies, criminology and law, health and the sciences, history, industrial and labor relations, social sciences, literature and literary criticism, philosophy and political theory, psychiatry and counseling, psychology, religion, sexology, sociology, and Third World studies. Indexes are included to cover interdisciplinary areas. See ordering address in #135.

167. Oakes, Elizabeth H., and Kathleen E. Sheldon, *Guide to Social Science Resources in Women's Studies.* Santa Barbara, Calif.: Clio Press, 1978.

An annotated bibliography of books and bibliographies developed for "professors of introductory interdisciplinary women's studies courses and those who wish to include material on women in other courses"; arranged by disciplines, including anthropology, economics, history, psychology, sociology, and contemporary feminist thought. Also includes sections on bibliographies, journals, and other resources, and subject and author indexes.

168. Safilios-Rothschild, Constantina. *Sex Role Socialization and Sex Discrimination: A Bibliography.* Washington, D.C.: National Institute of Education, U.S. Dept. of Health, Education and Welfare, 1979.

A comprehensive list of literature on sex role socialization and sex discrimination published between 1960 and 1974. Designed to provide researchers with "an interdisciplinary bibliography on the subject and . . . a sense of the 'developmental' trends in this area over the last two decades." Includes books, journals, speeches, convention reports, and doctoral dissertations in the disciplines of history, sociology, anthropology, literature, psychology, and economics. Arranged by author only.

169. Safilios-Rothschild, Constantina. *Sex Role Socialization and Sex Discrimination: A Synthesis and Critique of the Literature.* Washington, D.C.: National Institute of Education, U.S. Department of Health, Education and Welfare, 1979.

The companion volume to **#168**. Provides a "more selective bibliography scrutinized for methodological and substantive considerations and arranged by major content areas."

170. Schmitz, Betty, comp. *List of Non-Published Materials for Developing Courses and Projects to Integrate the New Scholarship on Women into the Curriculum.* Mimeographed. Bozeman, Mont.: Montana State University, 1983.

An annotated list of materials from curriculum integration projects, such as syllabi, workshop agendas, and reports that have not appeared in published form or are being distributed by professional organizations; prices and ordering information are provided. Available from the author, College of Letters and Science, Montana State University, Bozeman, MT 59717.

171. Schuster, Marilyn, and Susan Van Dyne, comps. *Selected Bibliography for Integrating Research on Women's Experience in the Liberal Arts Curriculum.* Mimeographed. Northampton, Mass.: Smith College, 1983.

A selected bibliography of research on women in the fields of anthropology, art, biology, classics, economics, government, history, literature, music, philosophy, psychology and education, religion, science, sociology, theatre, and Third World; divides materials into those designed for classroom use (books, essays, anthologies) and those designed for teacher preparation (critical works, landmark essays, review essays). Available from the authors, Wright Hall, Smith College, Northhampton, MA 01063.

172. Searing, Susan, comp. "American Women's History: A Basic Bibliography," Mimeographed. Madison, Wis.: Women's Studies Librarian-at-Large, University of Wisconsin System, 1983.

A "highly selective" bibliography "designed for both teachers of introductory courses in the history of women in the United States and for teachers of survey courses in American history who are integrating women's history into their syllabi." Divided into four sections: reference works, single-author studies of women's past roles in the United States, anthologies of primary sources, and anthologies of secondary sources. Excluded are works on a single group or class of women and works focusing narrowly on the women's suffrage movement and the evolution of feminism.

173. Stineman, Esther, with Catherine Loeb. *Women's Studies. A Recommended Core Bibliography.* Littleton, Colo.: Libraries Unlimited, 1979.

A bibliography of 1,763 sources in women's studies designed "to provide an annotated and indexed collection, organized around traditional disciplines, of English-language, mainly in-print publications that support research on women." Includes books "recommended as essential items that should be available to users" and is designed as an aid to total library collection improvement. Annotations convey the content of the work, its applicability to women's studies, its relationship to other works on the topic, and ordering information.

174. Stineman, Esther, Catherine Loeb, and Whitney Walton, comps. "Recent Sources for the Study of the Culture of Women of Color." *Concerns* 9, 3 (September 1979): 15–24.

A bibliography focusing primarily on literary criticism, but also including reference works and studies of the general social and cultural background of women of color in the United States, 1977–79; based on an in-house search of the University of Wisconsin libraries. Includes reference works, works on the social and cultural background, and critical works.

175. Sims, Janet L., comp. *The Progress of Afro-American Women: A Selected Bibliography and Resource Guide.* Westport, Conn.: Greenwood Press, 1980.

A bibliography with a focus on twentieth-century black women; lists books and articles on black women in journalism, medicine, politics, religion, science, theatre, and other fields, as well as works dealing with sexual discrimination, blacks in the suffrage movement, and black family life. Also includes special sections on black women's autobiographies, biographies, and recollections of female slaves, and a list of special collections on Afro-American women.

176. Terborg-Penn, Rosalyn. "Teaching the History of Black Women: A Bibliographical Essay." *The Women's Studies Quarterly* 9, 2 (Summer 1981): 16–17.

A bibliographical essay reprinted from *The History Teacher* 13 (February 1980) that reviews sources and resources for developing a course on black women's history or integrating black women into the existing history curriculum; includes works for use in both chronological and thematic approaches to black women's history.

177. Williamson, Jane. *New Feminist Scholarship: A Guide to Bibliographies.* Old Westbury, N.Y.: The Feminist Press, 1979.

An annotated bibliography of 391 bibliographies, resource lists, and literature reviews on women published in the United States since 1967; arranged in thirty subject areas including anthropology and sociology, art and music, economics, education, history, lesbians, literature, minority and ethnic women, philosophy, psychology, reference sources, religion, Third World countries, and women and development. Indexed by author and title.

178. *Wisconsin Bibliographies in Women's Studies,* 1977–. Madison, Wis.: Women's Studies-Librarian-at-Large, University of Wisconsin System.

A series of bibliographies on current topics in women's studies compiled from lectures and workshops sponsored by the University of Wisconsin-Madison Women's Studies Program and through reviews of the literature. Titles include, for example: "Women and Power: A Bibliography of Feminist Writings," "Women in Scientific and Technical Careers," and "New Reference Works in Women's Studies, 1982/83" by Susan Searing; "The Lives and Politics of Latinas in the United States: A Selective Bibliography" by Catherine Loeb; and "Lesbian Literature, 1980–1983: A Selected Bibliography" by Margaret Cruikshank. See also ##**146, 161,** and **172.**

13

Resources for Program Development

This section includes resources for use in program development, such as directories of model programs and consultants, guides for program development, and organizations that provide human and material resources. Materials and organizations selected focus on curriculum rather than on the status of women in higher education. Resource and research centers that did not have a curriculum or research component were excluded. Readers are referred to the WREI *Directory of Selected Women's Research and Policy Centers* (**#188**) and the National Council of Centers of Research on Women (#201) for more complete listings, and to the American Association of University Women's *Professional Women's Groups Providing Employment Assistance to Women* (#180) for a discipline-specific list of caucuses and committees concerned with women's status in higher education.

DIRECTORIES OF PROGRAMS AND CONSULTANTS

179. Allen, Martha Leslie, ed. *Index/Directory of Women's Media.* Washington, D.C.: Women's Institute for Freedom of the Press, 1984.

The tenth edition of an annual publication produced to aid in "networking among women, women's organizations, and women's media, nationally and internationally." Contains a directory of women's media groups arranged under categories such as periodicals, presses, speakers' bureaus, courses, library collections, etc.; entries are arranged in geographical order by zip code with an alphabetical cross-index. Also includes an alphabetical directory of media women and media-concerned women, cross-indexed by zip code and country. Available from WIFP, 3306 Ross Place, NW, Washington, DC 20008.

180. American Association of University Women. *Professional Women's Groups Providing Employment Assistance to Women.* Washington, D.C.: American Association of University Women, 1983.

A listing of 117 professional women's organizations and women's caucuses or committees of professional organizations; provides name of organization, address, telephone, and contact person. Available from AAUW, 2401 Virginia Avenue, NW, Washington, DC 20037.

181. Anderson, Owanah. *OHOYO One Thousand: A Resource Guide of American Indian/Alaska Native Women, 1982.* Wichita Falls, Tex: OHOYO Resource Center, n.d.

A resource guide for Indian communities and for the dominant culture to assist in locating consultants and advisors. Provides biographical briefs of 1,004 American Indian and Alaska Native women in eight professional fields: arts, business, communication, education, health, legal, science, and social work. Indexed by resource skills, professional specialty, tribe, and state.

182. Bogart, Karen. *Resource Directory: Organizations and Publications that Promote Sex Equity in Postsecondary Education.* Washington, D.C.; American Institutes for Research, 1982.

A companion volume to the *Institutional Self-Study Guide* (#88) that "describes selected publications and national resources that may be helpful to institutions seeking to address equity needs." Divided into two parts: (1) a selected annotated listing of publications, arranged by issue under the topics of student, faculty, staff, and social-educational climate, that briefly analyzes possible sex inequities and offers suggestions for addressing them; and (2) a list of selected national resources with name, contact person, population served, services offered, and brief description. Distributed by the Project on the Status and Education of Women.

183. *A Directory of Consultants on Transforming the Liberal Arts Curriculum Through Incorporation of Materials on Women.* Wellesley, Mass.: Faculty Development Consulting Program, Wellesley College Center for Research on Women, 1984.

A partial listing of names, addresses, and brief summaries of experience of prominent faculty and administrators with expertise in the development of programs to incorporate the new scholarship on women into the liberal arts curriculum; updated three times per year.

184. Mairs, Nancy, Diane Sands, and Jana Halvorson, comps. *Directory of Consultants in the West.* Tucson, Ariz.: Southwest Institute for Research on Women, 1984.

A listing of names, addresses, and brief summaries of experience of sixty-five faculty, scholars, administrators, and activists in the Western states "who have experience in assisting faculty and administrators to incorporate women's studies scholarship into the curriculum."

185. McIntosh, Peggy, with Katherine Stanis and Barbara Kneubuhl, comps. "Directory of Projects: Transforming the Liberal Arts Curriculum through Incorporation of the New Scholarship on Women." *Women's Studies Quarterly* 11, 2 (Summer 1983): 23–29.

Current listing and abstracts of forty-two programs designed to help faculty in traditional disciplines use the research and perspectives of women's studies to revise courses and curricula. Includes information on programs that sponsor conferences and disseminate materials. Also published separately by the Wellesley College Center for Research on Women (#210) and updated annually. An edited version of the 1984 edition is found in Part Two of this book.

186. Project on the Status and Education of Women. Association of American Colleges. *Minority Women's Organizations and Programs: A Partial Annotated List.* Washington, D.C.: Association of American Colleges, 1984.

An annotated list, organized by ethnic group, based on information received in response to a questionnaire distributed by the Project on the Status and Education of Women; annotations include a brief description of the organization, contact person, and address. Includes some organizations not specifically aimed at women but that address issues of concern to minorities in higher education.

187. Project on the Status and Education of Women. Association of American Colleges. *Selected List of Federal Organizations That Address Women's Issues (Revised).* Washington, D.C.: Association of American Colleges, 1983.

An annotated listing of twenty-six federal organizations that address women's issues; annotations include name, address, chief officer, and statement of mission.

188. Women's Research and Education Institute (WREI). Congressional Caucus for Women's Issues. *A Directory of Selected Women's Research and Policy Centers.* Washington, D.C.: WREI, 1983.

A directory that highlights the primary activities, research foci, and publications of twenty-eight centers that responded to a July 1983 survey conducted by the WREI (#212). Includes reference tables on primary activities, current and completed research projects, and selected areas of expertise. Available from WREI, 204 Fourth Street, SE, Washington, DC 20003.

GUIDES FOR PROGRAM DEVELOPMENT

189. Girard, Kathryn L. *Developing and Negotiating Budgets for Women's Programs.* Newton, Mass.: WEEA Publishing Center, 1979.

A guide to program development that explains various types of budgeting and includes information on securing funds, planning budgeting cycles, and preparing actual budgets. Includes basic references and guides for training others to develop women's programs.

190. Girard, Kathryn L. *Developing Women's Programs.* Newton, Mass.: WEEA Publishing Center, 1979.
A guide offering step-by-step directions for planning programs focusing on the needs of university women. Presents advice on assessing program needs, determining objectives, and selecting appropriate program approaches and activities.

191. Johnson, Liz, comp. "Selected Activities Using 'The Classroom Climate: A Chilly One for Women?'" Washington, D.C.: Project on the Status and Education of Women, Association of American Colleges, 1984.
A paper that describes various approaches, activities, and strategies used by postsecondary institutions in response to the 1983 publication of the Project on the Status and Education of Women on classroom climate issues (#77). Activities at seventeen institutions are categorized under institutional dissemination, programs and workshops, in-class use, and research, reports, and surveys. Contact information is provided.

192. Rubin, Mary, and the Business and Professional Women's Foundation. *How to Get Money for Research.* Foreword by Mariam Chamberlain. Old Westbury, N.Y.: The Feminist Press, 1983.
A comprehensive guide to research-funding opportunities for and about women. Provides a list of current grants and resources, information on how to locate potential funders, how to determine eligibility, and how to write the proposal and formulate a budget. Includes a bibliography of other directories and grant writing guides.

ORGANIZATIONS AND RESEARCH AND RESOURCE CENTERS

193. Black Women's Educational Policy and Research Network. Wellesley College Center for Research on Women, Wellesley, MA 02181. (617) 431–1453.
An organization founded in 1980 to develop a national network of researchers and policy makers committed to educational equity for black women, to identify research priorities, and to support research. Publishes a *Black Women's Sourcebook* containing information on black women's research projects, recent publications on black women, and black women's organizations. Director: Patricia Bell Scott.

194. Black Women's Studies Faculty and Curriculum Development Project. Wellesley College Center for Research on Women. Wellesley, MA 02181. (617) 235-0320.

A project aimed at promoting the development of new courses on black women in historically black colleges and to facilitate the redesigning of existing humanities and social science courses. Co-Directors: Patricia Bell Scott, Gloria T. Hull, and Barbara Smith. Contact: Margo E. Bradford.

195. Center for Research on Women. Clement Hall 339, Memphis State University, Memphis, TN 38152. (901) 454-2770.

A center housing a Research Clearinghouse to aid scholars, policy makers, and the general public in locating up-to-date information on both in-progress and completed research on working-class women in the South and racial-ethnic women nationally. Publishes a newsletter and a working paper series on Southern women and on the intersection of race, class, and gender. Also sponsors conferences and institutes on women of color in the United States. Director: Bonnie Thornton Dill.

196. Committee on Women in Asian Studies. Association for Asian Studies, Inc., 1 Lane Hall, University of Michigan, Ann Arbor, MI 48109. (313) 665-2490.

A professional membership society founded in 1941 to promote and conduct research on women in Asia. Sponsors regional meetings and conferences, provides a forum for networking, and disseminates a list of publications. Contact: Carol Jean Johnson.

197. Federation of Organizations for Professional Women (FOPW). Suite 403, 1825 Connecticut Avenue, NW, Washington, DC 20009. (202) 328-1415.

A federation that works to enhance the professional status of women, influence public policy, and exchange ideas and information. Sponsors seminars and conferences, research, publications, and networking activities. A publications list is available upon request.

198. The Feminist Press. Box 334, Old Westbury, NY 11568. (516) 997-7660.

Founded in 1970, the Press publishes books that have changed the teaching of American literature, as well as other materials of interest to individuals, researchers, and curriculum planners on the topic of women's studies. Offers a variety of informational resources, such as the annual Women's Studies Program listing, consulting services, and *Everywoman's Guide to Colleges and Universities.* Also publishes *Women's*

Studies Quarterly, **#145**. Co-Directors: Florence Howe and Maxine McCants.

199. The Math/Science Network and the Math/Science Resource Center. c/o Mills College, Oakland, CA 94613. (415) 430–2230.

An association of nearly 1,000 scientists, educators, engineers, parents, community leaders, and people from business and industry established to promote the participation of women in mathematics and science. The Math/Science Resource Center, established in 1978 and active at all educational levels, is the coordination center for Network activities. Contact: Jan MacDonald.

200. Multicultural Women's Resource Center. Information Systems Development. 1100 East 8th, Austin, TX 78702. (512) 477–1604.

A center established in 1978 to serve as an information clearinghouse and forum for networking; maintains a computer data base on women researchers, speakers, writers, and women in business of all cultures, races, and ethnicities. Data base includes bibliographies on women's studies programs and courses and on bilingual and ethnic heritage programs with curricula or components on women. Contact: Martha P. Cotera.

201. The National Council for Research on Women. Sara Delano Roosevelt Memorial House, 47–49 East 65 Street, New York, NY 10021. (212) 570–5001.

An independent association of established centers and organizations that provide institutional resources for feminist research, policy analysis, and educational programs. Programs include the National Data Base Project and state-of-the-art conferences on collaborative research themes. Established in 1982. A list of participating centers is available. President: Mariam Chamberlain.

202. National Women's Education Fund. 1410 Q Street, NW, Washington, DC 20009. (202) 462–8606.

A national information-sharing network that provides information on public policy issues for women. Provides packets of materials and resources on specific topics through a Resource and Technical Assistance Service (RTAS) available on a subscription basis. Executive Director: Rosalie Whelan.

203. National Women's History Week Project. P.O. Box 3716, Santa Rosa, CA 95402. (707) 526–5974.

A grass-roots project founded in 1978 to promote the rediscovery of women's history and the establishment of the national observance of Women's History Week, March 7–13; serves as a clearinghouse for resources and provides technical assistance to educators, community organizers, historians, and others. Disseminates a Resource Catalog describing materials developed by the project (curriculum guides, community organizing tools, audiovisuals) and relevant materials from other sources.

204. National Women's Mailing List (NWML). Women's Information Exchange. 1195 Valencia Street, San Francisco, CA 94110.

A computerized data bank of mailing labels of groups and individuals that have requested direct mail and information in specific areas. Labels can be sorted by geography, demography, or interest area.

205. National Women's Studies Association. National Office, University of Maryland, College Park, MD 20742. (301) 454–3757

Founded in 1977 "to further the social, political, and professional development of women's studies throughout the country, at every educational level and in every educational setting." Members belong to the national organization and to one of twelve regional organizations. Services and resources include an annual conference, discounts on major feminist journals, a newsletter, and support networks for teachers, students, and administrators in women's studies programs. Coordinator: Caryn McTighe Musil.

206. OHOYO Resource Center. OHOYO, Inc. P.O. Box 4073, Wichita Falls, TX 76308. (817) 692–3841 or 767–6050.

Created with support from the Women's Educational Equity Act Program, the Center works to increase the visibility of American Indian and Alaskan Native women. The Center develops and disseminates resource materials and publications (##165, 181), conducts research, serves as a clearinghouse for information, and conducts conferences and workshops. Director: Owanah Anderson.

207. Project on the Status and Education of Women. Association of American Colleges. 1818 R Street, NW, Washington, DC 20009. (202) 387–1300.

An organization that provides information about women in education, and works with institutions, government agencies, and associations to develop programs to improve the status of women in higher education. Develops and disseminates research and policy papers on issues affecting women students and employees. Compiles a list of professional women's organizations. Also publishes a quarterly newsletter, *On Campus With Women,* that provides current information on issues, federal policies, court cases affecting women as students and employees, and resources, programs, and grants. Executive Director: Bernice R. Sandler.

208. Racism and Sexism Resource Center. Council on Interracial Books for Children. 1841 Broadway, New York, NY 10013. (212) 757-5339.

A Center that develops, publishes, and disseminates instructional materials to combat bias on the basis of race, sex, age, class, and disability, such as fact sheets on institutional racism and sexism, checklists for evaluating curriculum materials, and multicultural curriculum units on equity issues. Materials range from kindergarten through adult levels. Also offers workshops to help educators detect and alleviate bias in learning materials and institutional practices.

209. Southwest Institute for Research on Women. Women's Studies Program, 269 Modern Languages, University of Arizona, Tucson, AZ 85721. (602) 621-7338.

A Center that promotes collaborative research on women in the Southwest or by scholars in the Southwest through conferences, workshops and professional development training. Areas of research expertise include older women, especially widows; minority women in the Southwest; and non-sexist, multicultural education. Currently oversees the Western States Project on Women in the Curriculum, a small grant program supporting curriculum integration projects in sixteen Western states (see Part Two, "Directory of Projects"). Publishes a working paper series and a bimonthly newsletter, *SIROW*, which carries information on scholars doing research on women in the Southwest, calls for research data, publications, grant opportunities, awards and fellowships, and conferences. Director: Myra Dinnerstein.

210. Wellesley College Center for Research on Women. Wellesley, MA 02181. (617) 431-1453.

A Center administering a Program on Education designed to "improve for women of all races and classes their experience as students, as teachers, as scholars, as administrators, and as legitimate subjects for academic study and scholarly research." The Center's Faculty Development Program has three components: a National Fellowship Program for scholars to write about incorporating the new scholarship on women into the disciplines, a New England Faculty Seminar Series with similar goals, and a National Consulting Program that provides matching funds for consultants to assist institutions in initiating curricular change projects. Program Director: Peggy McIntosh. The Center publishes a yearly directory of projects to transform the liberal arts through incorporation of the new scholarship on women (**#185**) and

a Working Paper Series. Center Director: Laura Lein.
   See also: Black Women's Studies Project #194.

211. Women's Educational Equity Act Publishing Center. Education Development Center. 55 Chapel Street, Newton, MA 02160. (617) 969–7100 or toll-free (800) 225–3088.
   A center that issues a catalog of resources on educational equity for educators and administrators, K-postsecondary, that were developed under WEEA grants and contracts.

212. Women's Research and Education Institute (WREI) of the Congressional Women's Caucus for Women's Issues. 204 Fourth Street, SE, Washington, DC 20003. (202) 546–1010.
   Established in 1977 to form "a critical bridge between researchers and policymakers concerned with issues of particular importance to women." Activities include identification and networking of research and policy centers, policy analysis, sponsorship of conferences and symposia, preparation of research reports and briefing sheets, and research projects. Publishes *A Directory of Selected Women's Research and Policy Centers*, #188.

213. Women's Research and Resource Center. Spelman College, Box 127, 350 Spelman Lane, Atlanta GA 30314. (404) 681–3643, exts. 359, 360.
   A center whose major goals are curriculum development in black women's studies; research on black women; and community service for black women locally and in the South. Currently houses a two-year project to integrate black women's studies into the curriculum at Spelman, Morehouse, Clark, Kennesaw, and Agnes Scott colleges. Also publishes a biannual newsletter. Director: Beverly Guy-Sheftall.

Directory of Publishers

ABC-Clio Press
Box 4397
2040 Alameda Padre Serra
Santa Barbara, CA 93103

Association of American
   Colleges
1818 R Street, NW
Washington, DC 20009

Biblio Press
Box 22
Fresh Meadows, NY 11365

R. R. Bowker Company
205 East 42 Street
New York, NY 10017

Clio Press
See ABC-Clio Press

The Feminist Press
Box 334
Old Westbury, NY 11568

Garland Publishing, Inc.
136 Madison Avenue
New York, NY 10016

Great Lakes Colleges
   Association Women's
   Studies Program
220 Collingwood, Suite 240
Ann Arbor, MI 48103

Greenwood Press
Box 5007, 88 Post Road West
Westport, CT 06881

G. K. Hall
70 Lincoln Street
Boston, MA 02111

D.C. Heath & Company

125 Spring Street
Lexington, MA 02173

Indiana University Press
Tenth and Morton Streets
Bloomington, IN 47405

The Johns Hopkins University
   Press
Baltimore, MD 21218

Jossey-Bass, Inc.
433 California Street
San Francisco, CA 94104

Kendall/Hunt Publishing Co.
2460 Kerper Boulevard
Dubuque, IA 52001

Kitchen Table Press
593 Park Avenue
New York, NY 10021

Libraries Unlimited, Inc.
Box 263
Littleton, CO 80160

Longman, Inc.
19 West 44 Street
New York, NY 10036

McGraw-Hill, Inc.
1221 Avenue of the Americas
New York, NY 10020

Macmillan Publishing Co.
866 Third Avenue
New York, NY 10022

National Institute of Education
Mail Stop 7
1200 — 19th Street, NW
Washington, DC 20208

National Textbook Co.
4255 W. Touhy Avenue
Lincolnwood, IL 60646

National Women's Studies
    Association
University of Maryland
College Park, MD 20742

W. W. Norton
500 Fifth Avenue
New York, NY 10110

OHOYO Resource Center
P.O. Box 4073
Wichita Falls, TX 76308

Pergamon Press, Inc.
Maxwell House
Fairview Park
Elmsford, NY 10523

Project on the Status and
    Education of Women
See Association of American
    Colleges

Routledge & Kegan Paul
9 Park Street
Boston, MA 02108

Schenkman Publishing
    Company, Inc.
331 Broadway
Cambridge, MA 02139

Southwest Institute for Re-
    search on Women
    (SIROW)
269 Modern Languages
University of Arizona
Tucson, AZ 85721

University of Alabama Press
Box 2877
University, AL 35486

University of Chicago Press
5801 Ellis Avenue
Chicago, IL 60637

University of Illinois Press
54 E. Gregory Drive
Champaign, IL 61820

University of Wisconsin Press
114 N. Murray Street
Madison, WI 53715

WEEA Publishing Center
Educational Development Cen-
    ter, Inc.
55 Chapel Street
Newton, MA 02160

Wellesley College Center for
    Research on Women
Wellesley, MA 02181

Women's Educational Equity
    Act Publishing Center
See WEEA Publishing Center

Westview Press, Inc.
5500 Central Avenue
Boulder, CO 80301

Women's Studies Librarian-
    at-Large
University of Wisconsin
    System
112A Memorial Library
728 State Street
University of Wisconsin
Madison, WI 53706

Author Index

Note: Numerals refer to entry numbers, not page numbers, in Part Three of this book.

Subject Index

Note: Numerals refer to entry numbers, not page numbers, in Part Three of this book.

FEMINIST CLASSICS FROM THE FEMINIST PRESS

Antoinette Brown Blackwell: A Biography, by Elizabeth Cazden. $16.95 cloth, $9.95 paper.

Between Mothers and Daughters: Stories Across a Generation. Edited by Susan Koppelman. $8.95 paper.

Brown Girl, Brownstones, a novel by Paule Marshall. Afterword by Mary Helen Washington, $8.95 paper.

Call Home the Heart, a novel of the thirties, by Fielding Burke. Introduction by Alice Kessler-Harris and Paul Lauter and afterwords by Sylvia J. Cook and Anna W. Shannon. $8.95 paper.

Cassandra, by Florence Nightingale. Introduction by Myra Stark. Epilogue by Cynthia Macdonald. $3.50 paper.

The Convert, a novel by Elizabeth Robins. Introduction by Jane Marcus. $6.95 paper.

Daughter of Earth, a novel by Agnes Smedley. Afterword by Paul Lauter. $7.95 paper.

The Female Spectator, edited by Mary R. Mahl and Helen Koon. $8.95 paper.

Guardian Angel and Other Stories, by Margery Latimer. Afterwords by Nancy Loughridge, Meridel Le Sueur, and Louis Kampf. $8.95 paper.

I Love Myself When I Am Laughing . . . And Then Again When I Am Looking Mean and Impressive, by Zora Neale Hurston. Edited by Alice Walker with an introduction by Mary Helen Washington. $9.95 paper.

Käthe Kollwitz: Woman and Artist, by Martha Kearns. $7.95 paper.

Life in the Iron Mills and Other Stories, by Rebecca Harding Davis. Biographical interpretation by Tillie Olsen. $7.95 paper.

The Living Is Easy, a novel by Dorothy West. Afterword by Adelaide M. Cromwell. $8.95 paper.

The Other Woman: Stories of Two Women and a Man. Edited by Susan Koppelman. $8.95 paper.

Mother to Daughter, Daughter to Mother: A Daybook and Reader, selected and shaped by Tillie Olsen. $9.95 paper.

Portraits of Chinese Women in Revolution, by Agnes Smedley. Edited with an introduction by Jan MacKinnon and Steve MacKinnon and an afterword by Florence Howe. $5.95 paper.

Reena and Other Stories, selected short stories by Paule Marshall. $8.95 paper.

Ripening: Selected Work, 1927-1980, by Meridel Le Sueur. Edited with an introduction by Elaine Hedges. $8.95 paper.

Rope of Gold, a novel of the thirties, by Josephine Herbst. Introduction by Alice Kessler-Harris and Paul Lauter and afterword by Elinor Langer. $8.95 paper.

The Silent Partner, a novel by Elizabeth Stuart Phelps. Afterword by Mari Jo Buhle and Florence Howe. $8.95 paper.

These Modern Women: Autobiographical Essays from the Twenties. Edited with an introduction by Elaine Showalter. $4.95 paper.

The Unpossessed, a novel of the thirties, by Tess Slesinger. Introduction by Alice Kessler-Harris and Paul Lauter and afterword by Janet Sharistanian. $8.95 paper.

Weeds, a novel by Edith Summers Kelley. Afterword by Charlotte Goodman. $7.95 paper.

The Woman and the Myth: Margaret Fuller's Life and Writings, by Bell Gale Chevigny. $8.95 paper.

The Yellow Wallpaper, by Charlotte Perkins Gilman. Afterword by Elaine Hedges. $3.95 paper.

OTHER TITLES FROM THE FEMINIST PRESS

Black Foremothers: Three Lives, by Dorothy Sterling. $6.95 paper.

But Some of Us Are Brave: Black Women's Studies. Edited by Gloria T. Hull, Patricia Bell Scott, and Barbara Smith. $9.95 paper.

Complaints and Disorders: The Sexual Politics of Sickness, by Barbara Ehrenreich and Deirdre English. $3.95 paper.

The Cross-Cultural Study of Women. Edited by Margot Duley-Morrow and Mary I. Edwards. $29.95 cloth, $10.95 paper.

Household and Kin: Families in Flux, by Amy Swerdlow et al. $8.95 paper.

How to Get Money for Research, by Mary Rubin and the Business and Professional Women's Foundation. Foreword by Mariam Chamberlain. $6.95 paper.

In Her Own Image: Women Working in the Arts. Edited with an introduction by Elaine Hedges and Ingrid Wendt. $9.95 paper.

Integrating Women's Studies into the Curriculum: A Guide and Bibliography, by Betty Schmitz. $9.95 paper.

Las Mujeres: Conversations from a Hispanic Community, by Nan Elsasser, Kyle MacKenzie, and Yvonne Tixier y Vigil. $8.95 paper.

Lesbian Studies: Present and Future. Edited by Margaret Cruikshank. $9.95 paper.

Moving the Mountain: Women Working for Social Change, by Ellen Cantarow with Susan Gushee O'Malley and Sharon Hartman Strom. $8.95 paper.

Out of the Bleachers: Writings on Women and Sport. Edited with an introduction by Stephanie L. Twin. $9.95 paper.

Reconstructing American Literature: Courses, Syllabi, Issues. Edited by Paul Lauter. $10.95 paper.

Salt of the Earth, screenplay by Michael Wilson with historical commentary by Deborah Silverton Rosenfelt. $5.95 paper.

The Sex-Role Cycle: Socialization from Infancy to Old Age, by Nancy Romer. $8.95 paper.

Witches, Midwives, and Nurses: A History of Women Healers, by Barbara Ehrenreich and Deirdre English. $3.95 paper.

With These Hands: Women Working on the Land. Edited with an introduction by Joan M. Jensen. $9.95 paper.

Woman's "True" Profession: Voices from the History of Teaching. Edited with an introduction by Nancy Hoffman. $9.95 paper.

Women Have Always Worked: A Historical Overview, by Alice Kessler-Harris. $8.95 paper.

Women Working: An Anthology of Stories and Poems. Edited and with an introduction by Nancy Hoffman and Florence Howe. $7.95 paper.

Women's Studies in Italy, by Laura Balbo and Yasmine Ergas. A Women's Studies International Monograph. $5.95 paper.

For free catalog, write to: The Feminist Press, Box 334, Old Westbury, NY 11568. Send individual book orders to The Feminist Press, P.O. Box 1654, Hagerstown, MD 21741. Include $1.75 postage and handling for one book and 75¢ for each additional book. To order using MasterCard or Visa, call: (800) 638-3030.